THE GRADUATE INTERNSHIP PROGRAM IN TEACHER EDUCATION

THE GRADUATE INTERNSHIP PROGRAM IN TEACHER EDUCATION

THE FIRST SIX YEARS

BY
JAMES C. STONE and CLARK N. ROBINSON

UNIVERSITY OF CALIFORNIA PRESS
BERKELEY AND LOS ANGELES
1965

UNIVERSITY OF CALIFORNIA PUBLICATIONS IN EDUCATION
ADVISORY EDITORS: C. W. GORDON, FREDERICK LILGE, M. V. SEAGOE,
J. C. STONE, J. A. R. WILSON

VOLUME 15

Approved for publication May 1, 1964
Issued January 29, 1965
Price, $3.00

UNIVERSITY OF CALIFORNIA PRESS
BERKELEY AND LOS ANGELES
CALIFORNIA

◆

CAMBRIDGE UNIVERSITY PRESS
LONDON, ENGLAND

© 1965 BY THE REGENTS OF THE UNIVERSITY OF CALIFORNIA

PRINTED IN THE UNITED STATES OF AMERICA

FOREWORD

THIS MONOGRAPH is the report of a significant experiment in teacher education. Starting with the first group of students in June, 1956, a program new to the School of Education at Berkeley was set up to prepare teachers for secondary schools. This new program differed from the "regular" program then in operation in a number of ways. Chief among the differences were utilization of an internship, a year of full-time teaching in a public school, as the principal means of acquainting students intimately with the classroom and with problems of instruction; admission to the program only of students who had received a bachelor's degree and who had had little or no course work in Education; the requirement of a contract for a teaching position in a public school with duties to begin the next fall; a summer program of teaching and related seminars providing very early direct contacts with the classroom, frequently by teaching high-school classes in the first week of the program; a serious effort to associate closely together theory and practice, to the profit of each; and relative absence of the lecture as a method of instruction in favor of seminars and conferences.

This new program, never intended to replace the "regular" program, was set up for two quite different purposes: (1) to increase the supply of secondary school teachers by tapping a previously neglected source, and (2) to identify ways in which the regular program might be improved, from experiences with quite a different program. Both of these purposes have been achieved.

The authors of the report are eminently qualified for this responsibility. Long students of teacher education and often teachers of future teachers, they have taken major responsibility for planning the new program, have directed it from its inception, and have suggested many of the creative ideas for improving the program from year to year.

I have said that this monograph reports an "experiment." Some readers, because of their usage of that term, may be disappointed that the authors make no comparisons of students in the new program and their effectiveness as teachers with students prepared differently. Actually, no such "control group" could have been found if one had been deemed necessary (as it was not). The University of California students in the "regular" program would not have served, for they were on the average five years younger than the students in the new program, they lacked the variety and extent of work experience common to the latter group, and, because of the prospect of being only remotely involved rather than almost immediately charged with full classroom responsibility, they were not equally motivated. In any case, use of the word "experiment" is justifiable, for the word should be interpreted broadly enough to include investigations like the present one, in which the purpose is to discover what happens when a new course of action is being tried out. Progress in education is still probably more dependent upon the collection of authentic facts than it is upon the comparisons of groups supposedly equal in all respects save the one under study.

WILLIAM A. BROWNELL, *Dean Emeritus*
School of Education

PREFACE

IN THE SPRING of 1956 the School of Education at the University of California, Berkeley, instituted a new and different program to prepare teachers. The "regular" program, like those in many teacher-preparing institutions, received students in their junior year or later and intermingled professional courses with academic courses, culminating in supervised teaching. This program still exists, though modified considerably, in the Berkeley School of Education.

By contrast, the new program was available only to students who had completed a bachelor's degree in the liberal arts and who had had no courses in Education. Other requirements, which will be explained later, made for a highly selected group who were to be prepared in a special way. Intern schedules involved (a) eight weeks in the 1956 Summer Session, working at the University Demonstration Secondary School in an Oakland high school; (b) a year of full-time teaching under contract and with pay in a nearby junior or senior high school, during which time some course work was taken at the University; and (c) ten weeks in the 1957 Summer Session, of which six weeks were in academic departments and four weeks in the School of Education.

From the start, these students, called interns, had classroom contacts, many of them teaching in the first few days of their first summer session, and, throughout, every possible means was sought to relate practice and theory.

This program, known as the Graduate Internship Program in Teacher Education, is now in its eighth year. When it was conceived, and subsequently as it developed, there was no intent to establish a basis for a comparative study of teacher education. A control group was never contemplated. The purpose of the Program has been to develop an alternate pattern of teacher education based on a teaching internship and suited to the preparation of a limited, specially selected group of mature candidates and to assess the effectiveness of this program in the preparation of good teachers. In bold outline, the original plan of organization still persists, but numerous minor changes have been made in the light of experience. It is the purpose of this monograph to report what has been going on in the first six years.

JAMES C. STONE

Berkeley
CLARK N. ROBINSON

CONTENTS

I. Genesis	1
II. Recruitment, Screening, and Selection	11
III. The Interns	19
IV. The Curriculum	37
V. The Intern as a Public School Employee	58
VI. Mobility and Permanency of Interns as Teachers	77
A Concluding Word	86
Appendix	90

CHAPTER I

THE GENESIS OF THE GRADUATE INTERNSHIP PROGRAM

THE GRADUATE INTERNSHIP TEACHER EDUCATION PROGRAM for the preparation of secondary school teachers was established on the Berkeley campus of the University of California in the spring of 1956. The genesis of this new experimental program can be traced to converging national, state, and University concerns with teacher education at that time.

THE NEED FOR MORE TEACHERS, BETTER PREPARED

Throughout the nation there was a shortage of teachers. In a review of the problems faced by the nation's schools in the 1950's, the shortage of able teachers was seen to be the major threat to the quality of education in America.

At all educational levels, indeed, the swelling enrollments produced the same physical problems: too few chairs per classroom, too few rooms per building, too few buildings per school, and too few supplies of all sorts. Although taxpayers groaned and protested, these were deficits in *quantity* that money could make up in fairly short order. But money could not make up the growing threat to the *quality* of instruction, the major cause of which was a severe and increasing shortage of able teachers. The growing student bodies of our schools would, in themselves, have made for such a shortage, but it was greatly worsened by the fact that teacher salaries had failed to keep pace with industrial pay scales. Some of the most able teachers left the schools; many students who might have thought of teaching as a career excluded it from their plans. The result was not merely undersupply, but a threat to the quality of education.[1]

In California, as elsewhere among the states, the threat of a lack of qualified teachers was critical. "The present ... shortage of teachers remains the greatest crisis facing public education," was the conclusion expressed in a California State Department of Education bulletin[2] reporting a study of teacher supply and demand in the state.

The best single measure of the demand for teachers is probably the size of the school population taught. In the mid-fifties, secondary school enrollments were increasing at a fantastic rate due to the wave of persons moving to California and to the "war babies" who were reaching high school age. The State Department of Education bulletin referred

---

[1] *Decade of Experiment, 1951–1961*, The Fund for the Advancement of Education (New York: The Fund, 1961), p. 13.
[2] James C. Stone, *Teachers for Tomorrow's Children*, Bulletin of the California State Department of Education, XXV, No. 2 (Sacramento: June, 1956).

to the recorded growth of public school enrollments to 1953 and predicted the growth to 1965. "It took California *90* years (1849–1940) to enroll *one million* pupils in its public schools, and *13* years (1940–1953) to enroll its *second million* pupils; it is estimated that within seven years (1953–1960), California will enroll its *three-millionth pupil*, and that *within five years* (1960–1965), California will enroll its *four-millionth pupil*."[3] These predictions, startling when made, have already proved to be far too conservative. The four-millionth pupil actually entered the public schools early in 1962.

The supply of teachers was diminishing during this period of growing demand, thus compounding the teacher shortage problem. During the four years of World War II, the number of students beginning preparation for teaching had fallen off to a mere fraction of those required. The four-year gap between the number of persons entering teaching and those needed in the classroom was not to be closed in the postwar years, for the vocation of teaching often could not compete with other careers which were more rewarding in terms of status and income as well as being psychologically less enervating than teaching. Consequently, the prospect for an organized teaching profession worsened in terms of both the quantity and the quality of its current and predicted membership.

Moreover, the inability of the public schools at that time to compete with other types of employment for qualified manpower led to increased turnover among teachers. Many of them, often the most capable, left the classroom for other fields of livelihood.

The discrepancy between the supply of and the demand for teachers in California had become exceedingly serious. To meet this emergency, the size of classes often was enlarged, and professional requirements for entry into teaching were reduced. Compromise solutions like the issuance of emergency and provisional credentials were necessarily put into effect, and many "unqualified" people were employed to staff California's classrooms. In the 1955–1956 school year 11,516 teachers, or 9.8 per cent of the total certificated personnel teaching in the State, were employed on substandard credentials. These figures from the State Department of Education carry increased significance when translated into terms of students taught by inadequately prepared teachers. "Assuming a median elementary class size of 34 and a secondary class size of 25, the number of persons serving on substandard credentials in 1955–56 are teaching an estimated total of 360,000 pupils."[4]

---

[3] *Ibid.*, p. 32
[4] *Ibid.*, p. 4

While these temporary, makeshift solutions just noted helped provide a teacher, qualified or not, for every classroom, they tended to lower the professional status of teaching and often dissuaded able people from entering a profession of diminishing prestige. Obviously, the emergency measures could not provide optimal solutions to California's need for qualified teachers.

The problem of how to provide enough teachers for the schools of the State became a matter of vital concern to the public, the teaching profession, and teacher-preparing institutions. In this common concern can be seen one important factor in the genesis of the University of California Graduate Internship Teacher Education Program, established in 1956.

EVALUATION OF EXISTING PROGRAM

Another factor leading to the establishment of an experimental program in teacher education, resulted from certain activities within the School of Education on the Berkeley campus. Some members of the faculty, encouraged by W. A. Brownell, then Dean, to examine critically the teacher education program, had been questioning the effectiveness of certain practices and suggesting the need for further study of the existing teacher education program. Indicative of this concern is a joint statement by two faculty members in 1954, titled, "A Few Thoughts on the Teacher Education Program at Berkeley."[5] Why were they concerned? Their first paragraph answers this question.

> For at least twenty-five years there has been no complete internal evaluation of the teacher education program at the University of California, Berkeley .... The need for a fundamental self-appraisal by the people in the School of Education is evident.

The writers then listed "various impressions" about the teacher education program in operation at that time, some of which they thought might warrant further study by the School of Education Committee on Teacher Education. Summarized, some of their impressions in 1954 were:

> The present system of lecture courses, many of them large in enrollment, may not be producing competent, creative teachers.

> The present courses largely are based on a lecture-homework system which transmits large quantities of factual material which seldom develops into operational understandings and skills ... In any discipline facts are needed, but they are probably learned best as they are used.

> The present pattern of required courses, followed by supervised teaching, tends to give students an acquaintance with theory first, some demonstrations of how schools

---

[5] David Russell and Walter Loban, unpublished report to the Teacher Education Committee.

and classrooms operate, and then some experience with the actual problems of teaching. This is essentially the reverse of many learning situations. It emphasizes results rather than the understanding of processes. It emphasizes "knowing all the answers" at the verbal rather than the operational level.

Because first-hand acquaintance with problems of teaching comes in the classroom, candidates should have such experiences in conjunction with their theory courses.

The present arrangement of college courses followed by supervised teaching is not only psychologically unsound in terms of the way one learns, but it creates an unnecessary gap between theory and practice.

Ten years ago, former students, too, were questioning certain elements of the professional curriculum by which they had been prepared for teaching. A study of the reaction of beginning teachers to their program of professional preparation at the University, completed at this time under the direction of the Field Service Center, tended to support the above impressions.

Thus in 1954 there was a questioning attitude prevalent among some members of the School of Education faculty. The time was ripe for experimentation. Having encouraged realistic reappraisal of the teacher education curriculum by the faculty, Brownell now proposed an experimental program from which might come some answers to the numerous questions being raised regarding a new way to prepare teachers and, at the same time, to increase the number of persons entering the profession. Under the chairmanship of T. Bentley Edwards, the 1954–1955 Teacher Education Committee[6] gave much of its attention to the development of broad outlines for the proposed program.

A new pattern of teacher preparation is not easily devised; the new never is, for old patterns of thought and action must be modified to make creative thinking possible. Minutes of the Teacher Education Committee meetings indicate that from extended give-and-take discussions the broad outlines of an experimental program gradually took shape.

FINANCIAL SUPPORT FOR EXPERIMENTATION

As the teacher shortage reached crisis proportions in the mid-fifties, few other problems facing the American people were given as much general attention. In screening applications for grants, foundations, began to look with favor upon requests for financial assistance in the establishment of experimental programs in teacher education. Of particular interest were proposals to tap new recruitment sources. Conse-

---

[6] Members of the Committee were: T. Bentley Edwards (chairman), Clinton C. Conrad, Mary C. Jones, Anne F. Merrill, John U. Michaelis, Karl E. Schevill, and William A. Brownell (ex-officio).

quently, when the University of California sought foundation aid in the establishment of an internship-type experimental program which would increase the supply of competent teachers as well as provide data hopefully to improve teacher education, financial assistance was given by the Rosenberg Foundation of San Francisco.

The convergence in 1956 of (1) a critical need in California for teachers, (2) the desire of the University of California School of Education at Berkeley to establish an experimental internship program, and (3) the willingness of the Rosenberg Foundation to support this effort were the major factors in the genesis of the University of California's Graduate Internship Teacher Education Program.

IMPLEMENTING THE INTERNSHIP PATTERN OF TEACHER EDUCATION

By June, 1956, the general plan for an internship program had been established. Board of Regent approval and financial support from the Rosenberg Foundation had been obtained. Three persons who would staff the project had been employed. Their assignment was to make the project experimental and broad enough to encompass the whole professional preparation of a group of secondary school teachers. It was to be a complete and largely self-contained program. Enrolling a group of qualified candidates having their baccalaureate degrees but no previous work in Education, the program was to include all those learning experiences needed to provide the professional competence required by the beginning teacher and to qualify members for a California general secondary teaching credential.

The three new staff members recognized the need for a consistent philosophical base for the experiment. Their task was not the development of new principles of education, but it was the reordering of known principles around the internship concept to create a pattern of teacher preparation which would supplement existing programs on the Berkeley campus, and, for selected candidates, to provide a parallel path into teaching.

The following are some of the principles around which the staff began to build the new experimental internship program.

The professional preparation of teachers should be a joint responsibility of the University and the public schools. "Preservice" education once marked the institution's responsibility for the preparation of teachers; "in-service" education was considered the school district's responsibility. Francis Keppel, formerly of the Harvard School of Education and presently U. S. Commissioner of Education, expresses the desirability of joint responsibility in this way:

What is needed is a way by which both the schools and universities can play more realistic roles in preparing teachers. We see the need of an arrangement similar to the relationship that exists between medical schools and teaching hospitals, where the medical staff contributes theoretical and research knowledge while the teaching hospital provides the hard-won insights of actual practice in the real setting.[7]

An internship program should pool the unique resources of the participating school districts and the teacher education institution in a way which might best discharge their shared responsibility to the beginning teacher.

The University's responsibility for the preparation of teachers should be shared by academic departments and the Education Department. Both breadth and depth in his teaching field should mark a teacher's preparation. With all of the professional work of the intern postponed to the graduate year, the internship program should free the prospective secondary school teacher during his undergraduate years for uninterrupted work in the liberal arts and in his subject fields. During his graduate year he would then be free to give his full attention to professional preparation for teaching.

Obviously, when approximately 85 per cent of a student's preparation for teaching is provided by academic departments of the University to assure *subject* competence, and when 15 per cent is provided by the School of Education to assure *professional* competence, the preparation of teachers must be viewed as a shared responsibility.

Theory and practice should be related to each other. The gap between "impractical" theory and "non-theoretical" practice in the preparation of teachers should be closed. Theory should be constantly illuminated and revised by practice, and practice should be genuinely inspired and guided by theory.

During both the preparatory experience and the full teaching responsibility of the internship, educational theory should feed into and be fed back by classroom practice.

Multiple programs of teacher education are needed within an institution. Persons vary widely in their personal characteristics, academic preparation, prior experience background, and motivation for teaching. Since there are wide differences in these respects among prospective teachers, a single pattern of preparation may not be suited to the needs of all who wish to teach. For example, some persons delay the decision to enter teaching and find it difficult and even impossible to

---

[7] Francis Keppel and Paul A. Perry, "School and University: Partners in Progress," *Phi Delta Kappan,* XLII (January, 1961), 174–180.

prepare through conventional programs. It may be too late for them to enter a professional program whose course sequence began during undergraduate years or financially impossible to return to the University to complete a credential program. For such persons and for other groups of prospective teachers, several programs may be needed. The internship pattern could provide a program better suited than others to the needs of some persons.

Experimental approaches to teacher education are needed. New understandings in teacher education, even after they gain general acceptance in principle, are not easily incorporated in the practices of conventional patterns of preparation. Realistically, it is difficult to test new ideas in traditional programs—indeed, even to give them a place in such programs.

The use of the internship pattern might free the staff to work creatively on a variety of problems in teacher education. To do so, it needs to be a self-contained program, permitting the staff to exercise considerable freedom in determining its elements and their relationship one with the other, as well as the particular manner in which each shall be implemented. The staff should be able to maintain the experimental nature of the program through built-in provisions for continuous evaluation of its features and their overall effectiveness. Two values should accrue from such evaluations: (1) provision of a basis for modification is made; (2) data of value to other programs of teacher education are gathered.

With these principles as the base for the new curriculum, early in 1956 the staff turned its attention to planning its structure. It would be a graduate professional program for carefully selected candidates having a baccalaureate or higher degree and, desirably, no previous courses in Education. Its emphasis would be on a close relationship between theory and practice. Professional study would be integrated with a limited period of observation and participation, including an intensive period of student teaching. A year of full-time internship teaching as an employee of a school district would follow.

In structure, the program being planned would consist of three phases: (1) the preparation for internship teaching; (2) the year of internship teaching; and (3) the post-internship experiences. Seminar study would accompany each phase. In the first phase, the intern would have supervised teaching experience; in the second, under the cooperative supervision of school district and University, he would assume full responsibility for a classroom by becoming an employee of a school district on a contractual basis; and in the third, he would complete academic and professional requirements for a California general secondary credential.

With plans for the new, experimental program completed and a group of 23 interns ready to begin their professional preparation for teaching, the Graduate Internship Teacher Education Program began operating June 15, 1956. An historical account of the Program to the present time will not be given here. The Progress Report[8] published in 1959 traces its development during the first three years. This second progress report will consider the current structure and operation of the Program.

While many minor changes have been made in its elements during the past six years, its basic structure as outlined below has remained the same.

GRADUATE PROGRAM IN TEACHER EDUCATION

ENTERING THE PROGRAM (late fall, winter, and early spring)
Recruitment—A candidate for the Program may
 1. Make direct application to the Program office, or
 2. Be referred by a school district interested in sponsoring and employing the candidate if he meets Program standards.

Screening and Selection—Candidates are given a dual screening
 1. Program staff screens applicants with baccalaureate degree, for:
   a. Personal and scholastic qualifications for graduate study.
   b. Appropriate subject matter background for a credential at the level and in the field in which teaching is contemplated.
   c. Personal fitness for teaching as determined by testing, references, interviews, etc.
   Successful candidates are tentatively accepted in the Program, final acceptance being contingent upon employment.
 2. School districts screen and select those to be finally accepted in the program by:
   a. Examination of applicant's placement papers.
   b. Interview of candidate by district officials.
   c. Consultation with Program staff.
   d. Employment and assignment to a teaching position.

PRE-INTERNSHIP TEACHING PREPARATION (first summer of Program)
Work in a Secondary Summer School (seven weeks)—
 1. The intern observes, participates, and teaches under the supervision of master teachers and the Program staff.
 2. Daily seminars conducted by the Program staff are concerned with problems of teaching and are related to the intern's teaching experiences. Attention is given to the preparation of lesson plans and materials for use in the internship teaching assignment beginning in the fall.

---

[8] James C. Stone, *The Graduate Internship Program in Teacher Education, A Progress Report* (Berkeley: University of California, January, 1959).

INTERNSHIP TEACHING (school year, September to June)
The Teaching Internship—This school year is the heart of the internship program of teacher education, providing
1. Orientation to the district and the school.
2. *A year of teaching experience in a regular classroom assignment with full responsibility.*
3. Cooperative supervision by school district personnel, University supervisors, and Program staff.
4. Scheduled Saturday seminars on the UC Campus conducted by the Program staff, centered on:
    a. Problems growing out of internship teaching experiences.
    b. Professional content to increase teaching competency.

POST-INTERNSHIP EXPERIENCES (second summer of Program)
Summer Study of Academic and Professional Subject Matter—
1. Work in teaching-subject fields taken from offerings of academic departments (first 6 weeks).
2. Intern workshop to complete professional content requirements leading to a general secondary credential (next 4 weeks).

Total—28 units

The Program has grown, and the source of financial support has changed. The number of interns enrolled in successive years—23, 55, 63, 60, 60, and 72—indicate the extent of the growth. The quota of 60 interns annually, set in 1958–1959, was increased to 75 in 1961–1962 to permit the acceptance of 15 candidates from the Mathematics for Teachers Program of the Mathematics Department. Gradually the University assumed full financial support and finally made the Program a permanent part of teacher education at the University of California.

A leaflet for distribution to applicants lists the minimum qualifications for membership as follows:

To be eligible, applicants must have (1) a baccalaureate degree from an accredited college or university; (2) few or no previous professional courses in education . . . ; (3) academic qualifications for graduate standing at the University of California; (4) appropriate subject matter background to meet credentialling requirements; (5) personal fitness as determined by testing, references, health examination, and interviews.[9]

Since the number of qualified applicants now far exceeds the established yearly quota, only the best candidates are selected. Listed minimum requirements, therefore, have limited significance.

During the past six years, screening procedures have been improved for the identification of the best qualified applicants. Much has been done to assure more selective placement of candidates in public school

[9] University of California, Berkeley, Department of Education, Field Service Leaflet No. 9.

teaching positions. Present recruitment, screening and placement procedures will be described in chapter ii. Some characteristics of the 333 interns who have completed the Program are discussed in chapter iii.

Within the Program structure, minor changes have been made from year to year in the curriculum to strengthen the preparation of intern teachers. The report in chapter iv gives a panoramic view of the curriculum as it now exists.

Plans leading to the establishment of the Internship Program in 1956 included provision for evaluation as an integral part of the Program. Its role was made clear from the beginning. However, evaluation was not to be the tail that wagged the dog. The Program was not planned to fit the rigid requirements of a pre-determined research design. Since an evolving program built around the internship concept was envisioned, it was important that the research design should in no way limit flexibility or prevent modification of any of the Program elements at any time. As the intent was to select for membership in the Program the most capable persons from those who applied, no effort was to be made to compare the Program's effectiveness with that of other existing programs of teacher education. There would be no "control" group. Research was to support, not control, the new program.

All those persons who have actively participated in the Program—interns, externs (former interns), staff members, master teachers, University and district supervisors, building principals, and other school administrators—have contributed to its evaluation. Instruments and techniques which have provided evaluative data include applications, official transcripts, tests, interviews, reference letters, grades, logs, intern evaluations, questionnaires, reaction sheets, observation reports, and assessments of teaching effectiveness.

What then were to be the uses of the data accumulated through these procedures? These data were to:

1. provide information regarding the characteristics of those who were accepted in the Program.

2. offer continuous feedback from the Program operations that would be helpful to the staff in determining needed modifications.

3. assess intern perceptions both for effecting changes in the curriculum and for developing the interns' habits of self-criticism and concern with pupils' responses in their own classes.

4. evaluate the teaching effectiveness of interns.

5. contribute to the literature of teacher education.

This report is based on the accumulated research data.

CHAPTER II

RECRUITMENT, SCREENING, AND SELECTION

From the outset, candidates for the Graduate Internship Teacher Education Program have been screened carefully. Only those persons believed to have high potential for teaching success are selected. High standards for acceptance are possible since the number of persons who apply each year far exceeds the quota of 75 to be accepted. High standards, always desirable in any program of teacher education, are essential in the Internship Program since school districts of the Bay Area employ its members before their professional preparation even begins. Indeed, a contract is a prerequisite to admission.

The identification and acceptance of the strongest candidates from the many who apply would be a simple matter if the characteristics of a good teacher could be clearly defined and if reliable, objective measures for selecting those candidates who possess these characteristics were presently available. Education, as yet, has not achieved either of these goals.

Well aware of these limitations, the Internship staff developed a screening process which minimizes them to a considerable degree. In place of one person's judgment of an applicant's qualifications, a composite judgment of all staff members and other persons is used. In place of one screening device, a number are employed.

Upon joining the Program, each staff member has come with his own conception of a good teacher, each conception evolving from differing experiences in education. Each staff member, competent in a subject field, has taught in the public schools. All have completed extensive graduate work. Experiences in school administration, supervision, curriculum development, and teacher education have rounded out their backgrounds. Each staff member's image of good teaching and of the successful teacher has become further sharpened as he worked closely with many interns during their entire period of preparation. The promise of an applicant determined during screening could be observed as it unfolded (or failed to unfold) during the Program. Thus, as the staff worked with successive groups of interns, members refined their conceptions of the potentially successful teacher who would be suited to the requirements of the Program and would benefit most from its curriculum.

In order to minimize recognized limitations of individual screening devices and procedures, several approaches have been used in combination to select candidates. In general, it is felt that the best bases for selection are the perceptions of a number of people who have known the candidate in a variety of situations over an extended period of time, and the use of a number of devices to assess personal and academic qualifications. The screening and selection procedures of the Program have evolved in keeping with this point of view.

RECRUITMENT

From the beginning, no aggressive program to recruit candidates has been necessary. However, there are many ways in which the Program comes to the attention of those who wish to enter teaching. Each year descriptive posters are placed on bulletin boards of the Berkeley campus. These posters also are sent to other colleges and universities in California, to city, county, and professional libraries of the Bay Area, and a number are made available to the California Department of Employment for posting in their professional placement offices.

Leaflets describing the Program and listing minimum requirements for candidacy are available upon request. Various professional journals and books which list experimental programs in teacher education have mentioned the University's Internship Program. A bulletin of the State Department of Education, *The Teaching Internship*,[1] names specifically the institutions in California which support internship-type curriculums in teacher education, and has had national distribution. *The Graduate Internship Program in Teacher Education, A Progress Report*,[2] published in 1959, has brought the Program to the attention of many persons working in teacher education.

Former interns speak about the Program to friends who are considering teaching as a career. Personnel in school districts where interns have been employed make referrals. Professors in academic departments of the University inform graduates interested in teaching of the professional preparation provided by the Internship Program. Counselors in the School of Education's Student Personnel Office present the internship path into teaching as one of the University's parallel programs leading to the general secondary teaching credential.

In recent years, more than 800 persons who have learned of the Program from these various sources annually communicate with the

---
[1] Dorothy S. Blackmore, Clark Robinson, and G. Wesley Sowards, *The Teaching Internship*, Bulletin of the California State Department of Education, XXIX, No. 9 (Sacramento: September, 1960).

[2] James C. Stone, *The Graduate Internship Program in Teacher Education, A Progress Report* (Berkeley: University of California, January, 1959).

Internship office for additional information. Records show that 44 per cent of these individuals phone, 29 per cent write, and 27 per cent visit the office. All receive the Program brochure and those who phone or stop by the office may ask for specific information. When requested, an application blank is supplied, accompanied by a bulletin which includes a brief description of the Program, requirements for candidacy, detailed instructions on how to make formal application, and essential facts regarding screening procedures. With this information, many possible candidates realize they do not meet minimum requirements, and so only 300 to 350 of them submit the formal application.

The fact that most of those submitting a formal application meet the minimum academic requirements of the Program indicates that there has been fairly realistic self-screening. Choosing the quota of 75 interns from the 300–350 people who make formal application is the purpose of the screening and selection processes.

SCREENING AND SELECTION

The selection of the 75 interns, who will begin their formal program of preparation for teaching in mid-June and enter classrooms of the Bay Area as full-time teachers in September, begins in October of the previous year. The entire Program staff participates in the screening and selection processes which continue until the Program quota is filled in early Spring. Although individual staff members may have major responsibility for particular aspects of the screening process, an effort is made to give each an opportunity to know every applicant at some stage of the screening process. This first-hand acquaintance is important since final acceptance or rejection of a candidate is by action of the entire staff and also since students accepted in the Program will be working with all staff members.

In actual operation, candidates move through screening in successive groups of 15–20 students. The date of application determines the composition of each of the five groups who pass through the screening process between October and March. Candidates who have submitted a formal application may be rejected at any of several stages.

A brief, chronological account of the screening and selection procedures for members of a group follows:

1. *Application.*—Formal processing begins when a candidate's completed application forms and transcripts of academic work are received in the Program office. In addition to personal information customarily procured, a candidate lists his high school, college, and community

activities; his hobbies; foreign travel; experience related to teaching; academic background; college distinctions and honors; and vocational experience. Further, each applicant is asked to respond to these questions:

How long have you considered teaching as a career?
What factors have influenced you in choosing teaching as a career?
What are the reasons for thinking that this program offers the best way for you to enter the teaching profession?
Why do you believe that you will become a good teacher?
At what grade level would you like to teach? Why?
Briefly, what are your career plans for the next ten years?

Obviously, no single response can be given too much weight, but an applicant's statements provide helpful information and, often, clues which may be pursued during later steps in the screening process.

2. *Transcripts.*—Official transcripts of all graduate and undergraduate work completed at accredited institutions are submitted by the applicant. On a form provided, he is asked to list courses in his teaching major, teaching minor, related courses, and courses in progress or proposed. In addition, he computes his grade-point average in major and minor fields. Not only is this analysis helpful to the staff members who must evaluate the transcript, but it also enables the candidate to decide whether he meets minimum academic requirements. Since the time when this self-analysis form was adopted, the number of academically unqualified applicants has been reduced to a minimum.

Transcripts are evaluated to assess the strength of the candidate's teaching major and minor fields, his breadth of academic preparation, and the recentness of his work, and to check his grade-point average. Clues indicative of an applicant's consistency of purpose and performance are noted. Those who do not meet minimum requirements are rejected at this time.

3. *Reference Letters.*—Each applicant submits a minimum of five reference letters written by persons who may comment regarding his promise for teaching in addition to supplying statements regarding his personal and academic qualifications. At least five of these letters must be from professors who have first-hand knowledge of the candidate's academic competence in his major field. For the successful candidate, these letters later become a part of his dossier on file at the Office of Educational Placement.

Reference letters are reviewed carefully by the staff. Despite the recognized limitations of such recommendations, they are felt to be of value in combination with other related information gained from a number of sources. What is said and what is not said, the consistency of the five appraisals, and clues that can be checked out in other ways—all these uses suggest the contribution and value of reference letters.

4. *Psychological Inventory.*—To give further insights into the applicant's personal characteristics and suitability for teaching, the California Psychological Inventory[3] is administered. Gowan,[4] Nelson,[5] and Hill[6] have reported research showing the CPI useful for the purposes in question. Through the use of this device by the Program over a period of years, its value has been enhanced as interns' profiles have been related to subsequent observations of their effectiveness in the classroom. From these observations, some general profile characteristics of the most successful and least successful teachers are beginning to emerge to serve as a guide in the interpretation of the profiles of current candidates.[7]

5. *Observed Interaction of Individuals in Group Discussion.*—Another assessment of applicants' qualifications is gained by having groups of six to eight discuss orally and extemporaneously a suggested topic having educational and personal significance. Seated around a table with two staff members present in the room but not participating, the unorganized, non-directed group spends a half hour discussing a topic such as:

> As a teacher you will work with a particular class for a semester or longer. What do you want to result from this relationship? You might consider both your immediate and your long-range goals.
>
> You are aware of the many conflicting viewpoints held by laymen today regarding the purposes of public school education and the best ways to accomplish these purposes. As you see it, what are the real issues underlying these conflicting viewpoints?

Observation of the individual's reactions in this group situation provides added insights into the candidate's qualifications.

6. *Personal Interviews.*—Of the several elements in the screening

---

[3] Harrison G. Gough, *California Psychological Inventory* (Palo Alto, Calif.: Consulting Psychologists Press, Inc., 1956).

[4] J. C. Gowan and May Seagoe Gowan "The G-Z and the CPI in the Measurement of Teaching Candidates," *California Journal of Educatonal Research*, VI, (January, 1955), 35–58.

[5] John Andrews Nelson, Jr., *The California Psychological Inventory as a Predictor of the Behavior of the Secondary School Teacher while Teaching* (doctoral dissertation, University of California, Berkeley, 1962).

[6] R. E. Hill, "Dichotomous Prediction of Student Teacher Excellence Employing Selected CPI Scales," *Journal of Educational Research*, LIII (May, 1960), 349–351.

[7] Richard V. Jones, *CPI as a Predictor of Teacher Effectiveness, A Preliminary Report*, unpublshed paper presented at California Education Research Conference, Bakersfield, California, March 11–12, 1960.

process, the personal interviews probably provide the most significant data. Candidates are interviewed separately by two staff members for a half-hour. To provide a common basis for comparative judgment, one of these staff members interviews all candidates, with responsibility for the second interviews shared by other members of the staff. The interviews yield further insights regarding the individual's personal characteristics, motivation for teaching, perceptions of the teaching process, understanding of adolescents, conception of the purposes of education, and, in general, his potential for becoming a good teacher. The interviewers at this time follow up any reservations developed by staff members in earlier phases of the screening.

7. *Selection by Staff Action.*—Tentative acceptance in the Program is the result of final action by the entire staff based on an evaluation of all the information which has been accumulated. All evaluations made throughout the screening process have been brought together and recorded on a summary form. When possible, these evaluations have been placed on a common 5-point scale. A rating of "1" or "2" is positive in respect to acceptance; a rating of "4" or "5" is positive in respect to rejection. However, final action is not determined by averaging the separate ratings. Each candidate is sponsored by a staff member at the meeting where final action on selection takes place. It is the responsibility of this staff member to be fully acquainted with all aspects of the candadate's qualifications and to recommend action. Each case is discussed until consensus is reached regarding the three possible actions—accept, reject, or hold for further consideration.

Usually there are some candidates who are clearly acceptable and others clearly not suited for membership in the Program: the former can be accepted quickly and the latter quickly rejected. But others may require added consideration. Some of these may be placed in a "hold" category to be acted upon later; thus time is allowed to obtain additional information on these candidates and to compare their qualifications with candidates in other subsequent screening groups. In some cases, candidates are asked to return for additional interviews.

Since the decision to accept or reject candidates from successive groups cannot be delayed until all applicants have been screened, a continuing problem is the need to make sure that when the Program quota of 75 is reached in March, those who have been accepted will be the best from the 300 who submitted applications. Further, the distribution by teaching fields of these 75 should fairly well reflect the employment needs of the coöperating secondary schools.

8. *Placement Orientation.*—Coöperating school districts have an important role in the screening process. Persons tentatively accepted by the Program must secure employment for the next school year in a school district of the Bay Area before they gain final acceptance into the Graduate Internship Teacher Education Program. Thus, the last screening is done by public school officials.

Two orientation meetings are held to prepare applicants for these meetings with school officials. They are told to register with the University's Office of Educational Placement and complete a set of placement forms and are informed to some extent about employment practices in school districts and about the organization, administration, and curriculum of the secondary schools. They are reminded more specifically about their Program commitments and the way these relate to their responsibilities to the employing district. Appropriate ethical practices related to employment need to be discussed. With so much to know and so little of it previously learned, the orientation meetings are invaluable in aiding the intern to find a position.

9. *Placement.*—Candidates who have moved successfully through previous screening procedures at last are ready for the final screening— employment in a coöperating school district. The total group now numbers approximately one-fourth of the persons who submitted applications some weeks earlier. Their activities are now centered at the University Office of Educational Placement. A roster of available candidates is mailed from the Program office to employing officials in all coöperating school districts. It gives each candidate's major and minor teaching fields, age, institutions attended, and degrees granted. Being familiar both with the candidates through the screening process and with the coöperating schools through supervisory activities in them, staff members are able to facilitate the placement of interns in several ways. Thus the staff works closely with the placement office, and serves as a liaison between districts and intern candidates during the spring employment period.

A new procedure used during the past two years has been so well received by employing officials and interns that it is now a continuing practice. Its purpose is to provide employing officials a preview of candidates, and to offer 75 candidates a preview of the coöperating districts. The geographic region served by the Program is divided into four areas. In early February, an evening "Pre-Placement" meeting involving intern candidates and prospective employers is scheduled for each of the four areas. Excerpts from the letter to districts outlining the purposes and procedures of the meeting follow:

> This evening is being scheduled to enable busy administrators of your geographic area to see a maximum number of qualified candidates with a minimum expenditure of time. You will meet only those candidates interested in finding employment in your area. We believe this meeting will be helpful to you in identifying those persons in whom you might be interested.
>
> Administrators present will be given a roster of the candidates, including pertinent information regarding each person. So that you can relate roster names with candidates present, they will introduce themselves. A social period will provide an informal opportunity for administrators and candidates to meet . . . . Interview rooms will be available for administrators who may wish to talk privately with specific individuals.

Immediate employment of a number of candidates takes place as a result of these meetings. In other cases, the contacts which are made facilitate the arrangement of later interviews, the visits of candidates to schools, and other activities which often culminate in employment. An over-all value, of course, is that it gives both administrators and candidates a better basis of choice. Right choices tend to place the intern in a school where his potential will be most fully realized.

School officials are not asked to give preferential consideration to intern candidates. It is clearly understood that an intern should be employed only when his qualifications are thought to be equal to or better than those of competing candidates. That they do compete successfully is attested by the fact that the same districts employ interns year after year, often early in the spring employment season. The teaching success of previous interns has marked the Program as a source of good teachers.

The screening, selection, and placement activities described in this chapter require considerable staff time from November to mid-spring. Is it time well spent? The staff is convinced that it is, and for several reasons. Certainly a program with a limited membership is obligated to select the best candidates available. On the basis of experience in selecting and preparing six groups over a six-year period, it is believed that an hour spent to assure the selection of a strong candidate saves many hours during the Program that might have to be spent with a weak intern. The former, with help, becomes the outstanding teacher; the latter, with maximum help, may fail, or at best become a mediocre teacher. Careful selection of members is felt to be a major contributing factor to the success of the Program, fully justifying the large amount of staff time it requires.

CHAPTER III
THE INTERNS

Mrs. Barbara Sullivan of the original 1956–1957 group of interns had been married a year when she entered the Program. She held a B.S. degree in home economics from Iowa State College and had worked for two years as a demonstrator for a foods company. After completing the first part of the Program, she interned as a home economics teacher in a city junior high school, remaining there for two years. Then she was transferred to a high school in the same district where she taught an additional two years, served as head of the department, and participated actively in the state home economics association. She resigned at the end of the 1961 school year because of pregnancy but says she plans to return to teaching as soon as her daughter is of nursery school age.

Frank Smith, of the 1957–1958 group, was married and the father of two children when he entered the Program. He had completed a bachelor's degree and a year of graduate study in biology at Stanford University. For three years he had been employed as a biologist for a research firm. As a member of the Program, he interned as a biology and chemistry teacher at a small rural high school; he taught there a second year, also serving as the assistant football coach. Then he transferred to a suburban high school where he has remained. He has completed his master's degree and has been awarded three fellowships by the National Science Foundation for summer study. He currently is the president of his local teachers' association.

Ronald Patton of the 1958–1959 group was a bachelor when he entered the Program. He held an A.B. degree from San Francisco State College with a major in political science. He entered the Program in June of the year he received his degree. His only previous vocational experience had been as a counselor in a private summer camp for boys. He interned as a social science teacher at an Oakland high school. Early in the fall of his intership year, he married a girl in the 1958 Internship Program.

Mrs. Virginia Newton of the 1960–1961 group, age 40, is the wife of a college professor and the mother of three teen-age children. Before being admitted to the Program, she earned a master's degree in chemistry and was employed as a research assistant at the University when she met her husband. She had been active in community affairs for fifteen years, president of an elementary school, a junior high school, and a high school P.T.A. unit, and had been to Europe twice during her husband's sabbaticals.

Four interns, chosen at random from the group of 333, have been briefly characterized. It is apparent from these short descriptions that members of the group differ one from the other; but they also have common characteristics. This chapter offers a statistical description of the total group of interns in terms of (1) the characteristics of the intern population as to place of birth, age, sex, and marital status; (2) their personal background; and (3) their academic preparation. All the analyses are of the time the interns entered the Program.

TABLE 1
PLACE OF BIRTH OF INTERNS

Year	Place of birth								Total
	California		Out-of-state		Foreign		Not known		
	Number	Per cent	Number	Per cent	Number	Per cent	Number	Per cent	
1956	10	43	6	27	0	0	7	30	23
1957	21	38	32	58	1	2	1	2	55
1958	24	39	31	49	4	6	4	6	63
1959	28	47	31	51	1	2	0	0	60
1960	19	32	37	62	4	6	0	0	60
1961	27	37	36	50	9	13	0	0	72
Total	129	39	173	52	19	6	12	3	333

CHARACTERISTICS OF THE INTERN POPULATION

The following facts related to place of birth, and the age, sex, and marital status of the interns were reported at the time they began the Program.

Place of birth.—Approximately 40 per cent of the interns are native Californians, 52 per cent were born out-of-state (but within the United States), and approximately 6 per cent were born in foreign countries. As shown in table 1, the proportions varied over the six-year period. Thirty-five different states are represented on the table of origins. The percentage of interns listing California as the place of birth varied from 43 in 1956 to 32 in 1960.

There is a noticeable increase in the proportion of interns of foreign origin in the more recent groups (table 1). Among all groups, 14 different foreign countries are represented. There were no foreign-born interns in the first year's group, one each in 1957 and 1959, four each in 1958 and 1960, and nine in 1961.

The geographic regions in the United States claimed by a sizable number of interns as their place of birth are shown in table 2. The West Coast Area (California, Oregon, and Washington) was reported by 42 per cent of the group, the Middle West by 21 per cent, the East by 16 per cent.

Age.—The median age for the 333 interns was 26, in contrast to 23 as the median age for beginning secondary school teachers in general.[1] While the range in median ages—from 25.5 to 26.5—in each of the six groups has been fairly narrow, the individual age range has been wide, eight of age 20 (the youngest) and 14 of age 43 or older. By contrast among beginning secondary school teachers for the country as a whole, 44 per cent were in the 20-22 age range and only eight per cent fell in the 35-40 or over age range.[2] Over the six-year period there has been an increase in the per cent of interns in their early twenties and their early forties, whereas the per cent in the in-between age groups has tended to remain constant. The distribution of interns by age is given in table 3.

Sex.—The ratio of men to women in the Program has varied from approximately half to two-thirds being women, but the over-all proportion has been 42 per cent men and 58 per cent women. By contrast, the U. S. Office of Education study found the proportion to be 59 per cent men and 41 per cent women in its secondary sub-group. In table 4 are shown the numbers and percentages of men and women and how these have varied over the six-year period.

Marital Status.—Two-thirds of the men and one-third of the women were married at the time they entered the Program. Marriages also occurred during the 15 months of the Program, often between interns or between interns and their school colleagues. Marital status at the time of admission to the Program is shown in table 5.

BACKGROUND EXPERIENCE

Prior to admission to the Program interns had an extensive range of vocational and travel experiences, hobbies, and work with school-age children. The variety of experiences of each year's intern group pro-

---

[1] *The Beginning Teacher: A Survey of New Teachers in the Public Schools, 1957-1958,* U. S. Department of Health, Education, and Welfare Circular No. 510 (Washington, D. C.: U. S. Government Printing Office, 1958), p. 5.
[2] *Ibid.*

TABLE 2
Place of Birth of Interns by Geographic Areas of the United States

Year	West Coast Number	West Coast Per cent	North East Number	North East Per cent	Middle West Number	Middle West Per cent	East Number	East Per cent	South Number	South Per cent	Foreign Number	Foreign Per cent	Not known Number	Not known Per cent	Total
1956	10	44	1	4	2	9	3	13	0	0	0	0	7	30	23
1957	21	38	6	11	15	27	8	15	3	5	1	2	1	2	55
1958	28	45	4	6	11	18	7	11	5	8	4	6	4	6	63
1959	30	50	3	5	13	21	7	12	6	10	1	2	0	0	60
1960	22	37	3	5	18	30	10	17	3	5	4	6	0	0	60
1961	30	42	2	3	11	15	17	24	3	4	9	12	0	0	72
Total	141	42	19	6	70	21	52	16	20	6	19	6	12	3	333

TABLE 3
AGE OF INTERNS AT TIME OF ENROLLMENT

Year	Age							Median
	19–22	23–26	27–30	31–34	35–38	39–41	43+	
1956	2	13	4	3	1	0	0	25.6
1957	14	16	7	8	6	2	2	25.9
1958	14	20	10	7	9	1	2	26.0
1959	13	18	10	9	5	2	3	25.5
1960	19	15	12	4	6	4	0	25.7
1961	17	18	15	11	1	3	7	26.5
Total	79	100	58	42	28	12	14	26
Per cent	24	30	17	13	8	4	4	

TABLE 4
NUMBER AND PER CENT OF MALE AND FEMALE INTERNS

Year	Men		Women		Total
	Number	Per cent	Number	Per cent	
1956	8	35	15	65	23
1957	21	38	34	62	55
1958	28	45	35	55	63
1959	21	35	39	65	60
1960	32	53	28	47	60
1961	32	44	40	56	72
Total	142	..	191	..	333
Average	..	42	..	58	..

vided a wide background useful in teaching and enlivened the seminars during the training period.

Previous Vocations.—The number of interns with previous full-time vocational experience by occupational groups is shown in table 6.

Of the 333 interns, 190 or 57 per cent had previous full-time vocational experience lasting a year or longer. The average length of time spent in the vocation was four years. The occupational category, "clerical and sales," was the group into which the largest number of interns fell (62 or 19 per cent), followed by "professional and semi-professional" (51 or 15 per cent), and "skilled and semi-skilled" (49 or 15 per cent).

One hundred forty-three interns (43 per cent) had no previous fulltime vocational experience. This number included housewives and those who entered the Progam direct from college.

In the 1960 and 1961 groups the number starting the Program direct from college increased markedly over the corresponding number in previous years' groups. To a considerable extent, this change was a result

TABLE 5
MARITAL STATUS OF INTERNS

Year	Men Married Number	Men Married Per cent	Men Single Number	Men Single Per cent	Women Married Number	Women Married Per cent	Women Single Number	Women Single Per cent	Total
1956	7	87	1	13	8	53	7	47	23
1957	10	48	11	52	8	23	26	77	55
1958	17	61	11	39	17	48	18	52	63
1959	10	48	11	52	17	44	22	56	60
1960	26	81	6	19	7	25	21	75	60
1961	24	75	8	25	22	55	18	45	72
Total	94	66	48	34	79	38	112	62	333

of the University's Mathematics for Teachers Program. Beginning in 1960, under the leadership of Professor John L. Kelley, then chairman of the Mathematics Department, this new program in the Department of Mathematics was designed to recruit and prepare prospective secondary school mathematics teachers. The program was designed to feed annually 15–25 mathematics majors directly into the Internship Program.

Travel.—One of the interesting aspects in the background of interns was their foreign travel. Although data on foreign travel were not specifically requested on the application form, a large number of interns volunteered the information. (Of course, many indicated intranational travel, but no record on its extent was kept.) The number and per cent of interns indicating foreign travel were:

2 (9%) in the 1956–1957 group   10 (17%) in the 1959–1960 group
5 (9%) in the 1957–1958 group   12 (20%) in the 1960–1961 group
6 (10%) in the 1958–1959 group   38 (53%) in the 1961–1962 group

TABLE 6

Number of Interns with Previous Full-time Vocational Experience Prior to Entry into the Program

| Year | Occupational category ||||| Number of interns |
	Professional and semi-professional	Managerial or self-employed	Clerical and sales	Skilled and semi-skilled	Unskilled	Farmers	
1956	5	4	6	1	0	0	16
1957	7	3	10	14	0	0	34
1958	10	5	12	9	0	0	36
1959	11	5	15	7	0	0	38
1960	7	5	8	9	0	0	29
1961	11	6	11	9	0	0	37
Total	51	28	62	49	0	0	190
Per cent of all interns	15	8	19	15	0	0	..

The reasons given by interns for foreign travel were duty with the Armed Services, education abroad, vacation travel, and service with the diplomatic corps.

Forty-six interns or approximately two-thirds of those reporting foreign travel had been to Europe. The number of interns traveling to

TABLE 7
HOBBIES IN WHICH SIX OR MORE INTERNS PARTICIPATED

Hobbies	Number of interns	Hobbies	Number of interns
Attending art exhibits	17	Public speaking	8
Bridge	12	Reading	35
Camping	18	Sailing	15
Chess	7	Sculpture	11
Cooking	20	Sewing	30
Crafts	10	Sports	
Creative writing	13	Badminton	7
Cycling	8	Baseball	23
Dramatics	17	Bowling	15
Drawing	9	Dancing: folk and social	16
Fishing	15	Golf	16
Gardening	8	Gymnastics	9
Hunting	9	Hiking	9
Knitting	18	Skiing: water and snow	6
Movies	13	Softball	24
Music: listening, singing, and playing	27	Swimming	14
		Tennis	17
Painting	25	Volley ball	13
Photography	11	Travel	15
Plays	10	Woodworking	9

other areas was sixteen in Asia, four in Africa, four in Mexico, two in Canada, and one in South America.

The number of interns who had traveled abroad increased steadily with each successive year's group. There was an especially sharp increase in the 1961 class, with over half having traveled to a foreign country. There is reason to believe that the number with foreign travel may be even larger than the reported figure, since, as has been stated already, information on this point was not specifically requested at the time of application. Men who had been in the Armed Services for whom foreign travel is a regular form of assigned duty were not likely to report this as "travel."

Hobbies.—Most interns listed three or four hobbies, with a wide variety represented in the total group. The 38 more common hobbies (table 7) extended from aesthetic interests such as attending concerts and the theater to sports such as baseball, tennis, and weight lifting. The 37 less common hobbies (table 8) included such pursuits as prospecting, flower arranging, and taxidermy.

TABLE 8
Hobbies in Which Five or Less Interns Participated

Hobbies	Number of interns	Hobbies	Number of interns
Amateur radio	2	Model building	3
Astronomy	1	Mountaineering	5
Auto repairing	4	Nature study	3
Ballet	5	Prospecting	1
Bird watching	1	Puppets	1
Book binding	1	Puzzles	1
Ceramics	5	Rock collecting	2
Collecting coins and art prints	3	Rug making	1
Conservation	1	Scrabble	1
Copper enameling	1	Sports	
Dog training	2	Archery	5
Flower arranging	2	Judo	3
Fly tying	3	Ping pong	3
Flying	4	Skating, ice	4
Furniture design	3	Sports car racing	1
Gun collecting	2	Weight lifting	5
Home laboratory experiments	3	Stock market speculation	1
Indian lore	1	Tropical fish	2
Inventing toys	1	Taxidermy	1

Experience With School-Age Children.—Approximately 90 per cent of the interns had experience with school-age children prior to their enrollment in the Program, and many of them had worked with several youth groups. Of the 299 interns entering the Program with such experience (table 9), 22 per cent had served as leaders of church-associated youth groups, and 22 per cent had been counselors in boys or girls clubs. Serving as a counselor at a Scout camp, the "Y," or in private boys' and girls' camps was a summer occupation for 15 per cent, and 11 per cent had worked as recreation leaders.

Thirty per cent of the total group had teaching experience of varying kinds and amounts. In this 30 per cent were 63 interns who had served as a teaching assistant in a college or university, 43 interns who had been tutors, 31 who taught in the Armed Services, 11 in nursery schools, and 7 in business schools. Five had been private music teachers.

ACADEMIC PREPARATION

The academic preparation of the intern may be described by noting the institution from which he received his bachelor's degree; his major and minor field of study; his undergraduate grade-point average; and

TABLE 9
PREVIOUS EXPERIENCE OF INTERNS WITH YOUTH GROUPS

Youth group activities	Number	Per cent
Church associated groups	116	22
Club counselors	115	22
Camp counselors	77	15
Teaching (in an educational institution)	63	12
Recreation leader	58	11
Tutoring	43	8
Military training	31	6
Nursery School	11	2
Business training	7	1
Music lessons	5	1
Total	526	100

the amount, kind and quality of the graduate academic work he had completed before entering the Program.

Bachelor's Degrees.—All interns held at least a bachelor's degree at the time they entered the Program, whereas only 58 per cent of all beginning secondary school teachers in the United States were reported to have reached this point by the time they commenced teaching.[3] The number and per cent of interns receiving their bachelor's degrees from various colleges and universities are summarized in table 10. The University of California (state-wide) was the baccalaureate institution for 43 per cent of the interns, California private colleges and universities for 16 per cent, California state colleges for 8 per cent, and foreign institutions for 2 per cent. Institutions outside California but within the United States had granted the bachelor's degree to the remaining 30 per cent.

Within the University of California, the number from each of the various campuses was as follows: Berkeley, 134; Davis, 3; Los Angeles,

[3] *Ibid.*, p. 11.

TABLE 10

Number and Per Cent of Interns Who Earned Their Bachelor's Degrees in Various Colleges and Universities

| Year | Institutions ||||||||| Total |
| | University of California || California state colleges || California private institutions || Out-of-state colleges and universities || Foreign institutions |||
	Number	Per cent	Number	Per cent	Number	Per cent	Number	Per cent	Number	Per cent	
1956	13	57	2	8	3	13	5	22	0	0	23
1957	26	47	6	12	9	16	14	25	0	0	55
1958	27	43	3	5	14	22	16	25	3	5	63
1959	25	42	3	5	9	15	23	38	0	0	60
1960	24	40	6	10	11	18	18	30	1	2	60
1961	28	39	8	11	8	11	25	35	3	4	72
Total	143	42.9	28	8.4	54	16.2	101	30.4	7	2.1	333

TABLE 11

NUMBER AND PER CENT OF INTERNS WITH MAJORS IN VARIOUS TEACHING FIELDS

Teaching fields

Year	Art Number	Art Per cent	Bus. adm. Number	Bus. adm. Per cent	Eng. Number	Eng. Per cent	For. lang. Number	For. lang. Per cent	Home econ. Number	Home econ. Per cent	Life sci. Number	Life sci. Per cent	Math Number	Math Per cent	Music Number	Music Per cent	Girls' P.E. Number	Girls' P.E. Per cent	Phy. sci. Number	Phy. sci. Per cent	Soc. sci. Number	Soc. sci. Per cent	Speech Number	Speech Per cent	Total Number	Total Per cent
1956	1	4	2	10	1	4	1	4	6	26	3	13	2	10	1	4	1	4	3	13	1	4	1	4	23	100
1957	6	11	7	13	4	7	3	5	6	11	12	22	5	9	0	0	3	5	4	8	5	9	0	0	55	100
1958	2	3	4	6	15	24	3	5	3	5	4	6	4	6	0	0	1	2	11	17	15	24	1	2	63	100
1959	3	5	3	5	15	25	5	8	5	8	3	5	4	7	1	2	2	3	4	7	13	22	2	3	60	100
1960	0	0	3	5	13	21	9	15	1	2	6	10	7	12	1	2	3	5	4	7	13	21	0	0	60	100
1961	1	1	3	4	17	23	10	14	2	3	3	4	12	17	0	0	1	1	7	10	15	22	1	1	72	100
Total	13		22		65		31		23		31		34		3		11		33		62		5		333	
Per cent		4		7		20		9		7		9		10		1		3		9		19		2		100

3; and Santa Barbara, 3. Other individual colleges and universities from which a sizable number of interns had received their bachelor's degrees were Stanford (20), San Jose State and Pomona (10 each), Occidental (8), San Francisco State (7), and Mills (6).

Academic Majors.—The academic majors of the interns were widely distributed among subject matter fields (table 11). Since the Internship Program was initiated in part as an answer to the shortage of teachers—particularly in such fields as mathematics, the sciences, foreign languages, English, girls' physical education and home economics—it is noteworthy that over two-thirds of the interns had majored in these fields.

Of the 333 interns in the six-year period of this report, approximately one-fifth had majored in the field of English, one-fifth in social sciences, one-tenth in each of the fields of mathematics, the life sciences, the physical sciences, and foreign languages.

The range in the number of semester units taken in a major field was from the State credential minimum of 36 semester hours to 69. The average number of semester hours completed in the major was 52. Those interns with majors in home economics, social sciences, and English tended to have taken the highest number of units (59 to 65 in these fields); those in the fields of mathematics, speech, and physical education, the lowest (41 to 43).

Academic Minors.—Like the academic majors completed by interns, the minors also were widely distributed among the teaching fields (table 12). Over one-third had minored in the social sciences, a fifth in English, and a tenth in each of the physical sciences, mathematics, and foreign languages. The subject matter areas in which there was an acute shortage of qualified personnel (mathematics, science, foreign languages, girls' physical education, and home economics) were the minor fields of preparation for 55 per cent of the group.

Undergraduate Grade-Point Average.—The quality of academic preparation in part is reflected by interns' undergraduate grade-point averages. The grade-point distribution by number and per cent of interns is given in table 13. Approximately two-thirds of the group had undergraduate averages of B or better at the time they entered the Program. The mean undergraduate grade-point average for the 333 interns was 3.14, on the 4-point scale.

Grade-Point Average in Undergraduate Major.—In the undergraduate major field, the mean grade-point average of the 333 interns was 3.05; for men it was 3.01; for women, 3.07. The 1956 ("pilot") group

TABLE 12

NUMBER AND PER CENT OF INTERNS WITH MINORS IN VARIOUS TEACHING FIELDS

Teaching fields

Year	Art Number	Art Per cent	Bus. adm. Number	Bus. adm. Per cent	Eng. Number	Eng. Per cent	For. lang. Number	For. lang. Per cent	Home econ. Number	Home econ. Per cent	Life sci. Number	Life sci. Per cent	Math Number	Math Per cent	Music Number	Music Per cent	Girls' P.E. Number	Girls' P.E. Per cent	Phy. sci. Number	Phy. sci. Per cent	Soc. sci. Number	Soc. sci. Per cent	Speech Number	Speech Per cent	Total Number	Total Per cent
1956	1	4	1	4	2	10	0	0	0	0	4	17	1	4	0	0	0	0	4	17	10	44	0	0	23	100
1957	1	2	1	2	7	13	3	5	0	0	2	4	7	13	0	0	1	2	12	21	19	34	2	4	55	100
1958	1	2	3	5	11	17	6	9	1	2	5	8	7	10	1	2	0	0	3	5	24	38	1	2	63	100
1959	2	3	0	0	12	21	2	3	0	0	5	8	5	8	0	0	0	0	8	13	26	44	0	0	60	100
1960	1	2	1	2	12	20	8	13	0	0	4	7	6	10	1	2	1	2	5	8	19	31	2	3	60	100
1961	2	3	3	4	16	23	11	15	0	0	1	1	5	7	1	5	1	5	6	8	26	38	0	0	72	100
Total	8		9		60		30		1		21		31		3		3		38		124		5		333	
Per cent		2		3		18		9		1		6		9		1		1		11		37		2			100

TABLE 13
UNDERGRADUATE GRADE-POINT AVERAGES OF ALL INTERNS

Undergraduate grade-point average	Number	Per cent
3.91–4.00	4	1
3.71–3.90	30	9
3.51–3.70	33	10
3.31–3.50	54	16
3.11–3.30	52	16
2.91–3.10	53	16
2.71–2.90	53	16
2.51–2.70	31	9
2.31–2.50	23	7
Total	333	100

TABLE 14
MAJOR FIELD UNDERGRADUATE GRADE-POINT AVERAGES BY SEX

Year	Men	Women	Average[a]
1956	2.55	2.45	2.49
1957	2.65	2.73	2.70
1958	3.06	3.17	3.13
1959	3.34	3.20	3.25
1960	3.08	3.25	3.15
1961	3.02	3.16	3.10
Average	3.01	3.07	3.05

[a] Averages were computed separately for both men and women, then recomputed on the basis of the total year's group. The over-all average was recomputed for the entire intern group over the six-year period.

had the lowest mean grade-point average (2.49), and the 1959, the highest (3.25). The low average of the 1956 group is explained by the fact that they were admitted after a short period of selection and publicity and before the Program staff reported for duty and had established the screening standards and procedures used in the selection of subsequent groups. With the exception of the 1956 and 1957 groups, all others averaged 3.09 or better (table 14).

Undergraduate Honors.—The number of undergraduate honors and distinctions claimed by interns is shown in table 15. These included honor societies (such as Phi Beta Kappa), scholarships, fellowships, Dean's lists, commencement recognition and similar distinctions. The data in table 15 are taken from the 1958 through 1961 intern groups, totaling 255 interns. Such information was not specifically requested in 1956 and 1957. Staff members, however, recall four in the 1956 group and five in the 1957 group who had received such recognitions. Among the 255 interns, 302 honors and awards for academic distinctions were listed: 36 Phi Beta Kappa members; 48 graduates with academic distinctions; 47 Honor Society members (exclusive of Phi Beta Kappa); and 70 Scholarship or fellowship holders. Some interns

TABLE 15

NUMBER OF UNDERGRADUATE HONORS AND DISTINCTIONS CLAIMED BY INTERNS

Intern class	Number of interns	Number of honors claimed
1958	63	71
1959	60	76
1960	60	59
1961	72	96
Total	255	302

claimed no distinctions. On the other hand, a number listed more than one award. One University of California (Berkeley) graduate, for example, received election to honors at entrance, Panile, Sophomore Women's Honor Society, Prytanean, Junior-Senior Women's Honor Society, Mortar Board, Senior Women's Honor Society, President Kerr's California Club, Robert Gordon and Ida Sproul Award for the outstanding junior girl, and Phi Beta Kappa.

Another intern was a National Merit scholar, member of Mortar Board, member of Alpha Mu Gamma, winner of the Maes travel scholarship, winner of the Pipal Scholarship, winner of the AMG scholarship, exchange student to Madrid, Phi Beta Kappa, second in graduating class, first woman, Fulbright scholarships to Vienna and Berlin, and Woodrow Wilson Fellow.

The following scholastic distinctions were reported by another intern: graduated with distinction in all subjects and with high honors in government, Mortar Board, Dean's list, Phi Kappa Phi, and Raven and Serpent. Another intern's distinctions were Pi Gamma Mu, Alpha Psi Omega, University Service Award, Arrowhead Award, Outstanding Future Officer Candidate, Dean's Honor Roll, and graduate *cum laude*.

Graduate Work.—Graduate degrees were held by 13 per cent (44 interns, table 16), who had completed a mean of 45.5 graduate semes-

TABLE 16

GRADUATE WORK COMPLETED AND GRADE POINT AVERAGES
OF INTERNS WITH HIGHER DEGREES

Year	Number of master's or higher degrees held	Average number of graduate units completed by interns who held master's degrees	Mean graduate grade-point average
1956	..	..	....
1957	..	..	....
1958	9	48	3.67
1959	11	43	3.42
1960	16	46	3.46
1961	8	45	3.29
Total	44	45.5	3.46

TABLE 17

GRADUATE WORK COMPLETED AND GRADE POINT AVERAGES
OF INTERNS WITHOUT HIGHER DEGREES

Year	Number of interns with graduate units but no degree	Average number of graduate units completed	Mean graduate grade-point average
1956	..	..	....
1957	..	..	....
1958	9	28	3.09
1959	15	19	3.11
1960	7	21	3.31
1961	16	18	3.37
Total	47	21.5	3.22

ter units with a B+ average on entrance to the Program. As would be expected for such a select group, this percentage is well in excess of the 5 per cent of beginning teachers shown by a national survey to hold a master's or higher degree.[4] By far the greater number of graduate degrees earned were in the social sciences (12), English (9), and foreign languages (5). The University of California, Berkeley, granted over half of all graduate degrees earned.

Graduate work without the receipt of a master's degree, averaging 21.5 semester units per intern, was completed by 47 prior to admission to the Program (table 17).[5] Their mean grade-point average was 3.22.

[4] *Ibid.*, p. 12.
[5] Graduate work as used in this report consists of courses completed following the receipt of the bachelor's degree.

English, followed by the social sciences (chiefly history), and foreign languages were the fields in which a sizable number of the interns took graduate work. The Berkeley campus of the University of California was the choice of a majority of interns as the institution for graduate work; 31 interns completed such work at the University of California prior to admission to the Program.

In substance, then, prior to acceptance into the Program, 91 of the 333 interns had taken an average of 38.5 semester hours of graduate academic courses, earning a mean grade-point of 3.34. Well over half of the interns (56) had taken this work at the University's Berkeley campus. The reader should keep in mind that the Program itself required these interns to complete, in addition, 22 units in professional education and 6 post graduate units in the major or minor teaching fields.

SUMMARY

Forty per cent of the 333 interns who have been in the Graduate Internship Teacher Education Program were born in California; their median age at the time of entry into the Program was 26 years in comparison with a median age of 23 for beginning secondary teachers throughout the nation. Fifty-eight per cent of the interns were women, one-third of whom were married. By contast, two-thirds of the men were married at the time they began the Program.

Over half the group had previous full-time vocational experience, on the average amounting to four years. Approximately nine out of ten of the interns had worked with children in a variety of capacities prior to seeking a career in teaching.

All had completed at least a bachelor's degree, 43 per cent from the University of California and 57 per cent from other colleges and universities throughout the United States. English and the social sciences were the most frequently presented academic majors. The mean undergraduate grade-point average of the 333 was slightly more than a B, and a sizable number were the recipients of academic honors and distinctions.

Slightly less than a third had completed various amounts of graduate academic work. Forty-four had won advanced degrees by the time they applied for admission to the Program, and 47 had completed varying amounts of graduate academic work but without the receipt of an advanced degree.

It is apparent therefore, that interns came into the Program with a varied background of vocational and avocational experiences and with a scholarly academic record.

Chapter IV
THE CURRICULUM

The curriculum of the Graduate Internship Program as described in this chapter depicts the main types of learning experiences which have been provided for its members. These experiences have come from two sources, those planned especially for the interns and those called for by the traditional professional content of Education. In developing the Program curriculum, the staff was continually concerned that these two sources of experience be integrated into an effective unity (fig. 1).

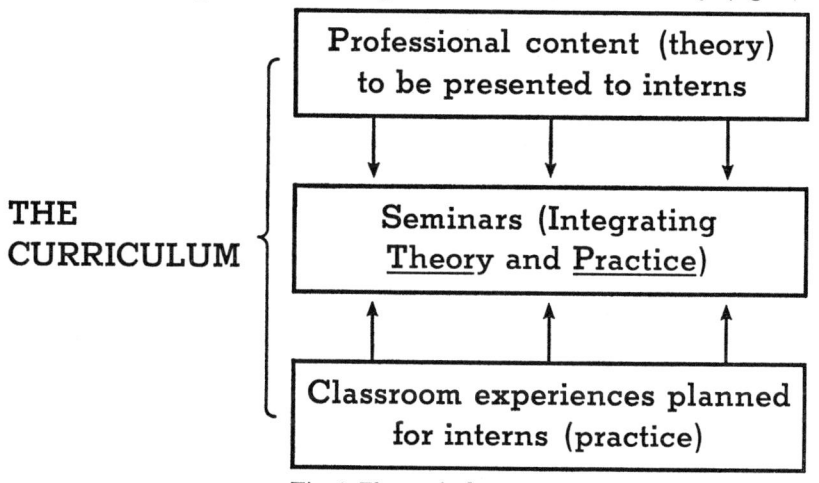

THE CURRICULUM
- Professional content (theory) to be presented to interns
- Seminars (Integrating Theory and Practice)
- Classroom experiences planned for interns (practice)

Fig. 1. The curriculum.

A member of the Graduate Internship Program is both a teacher and a learner. As he teaches, he learns: as he learns, he becomes a better teacher. Neither teaching experience nor related professional content, alone, is adequate as a curriculum for him; but when "practice" and "theory" are interwoven and interrelated, the contribution of each to the intern's professional growth should be greatly increased.

The intern makes immediate and direct contact with the problems of teaching as he teaches. Each day he has this laboratory experience, for he teaches throughout his program of preparation. Concurrently, he attends seminars and has other teaching-oriented experiences. This "practice" and "theory" must be related to each other throughout the Program, and both must be related continually to the intern's growing professional skills and understandings. In developing the Program curriculum, therefore, the staff has had to:

1. Provide a sequence of teaching and teaching-related experiences for the interns.
2. Select and organize an appropriate body of professional content.
3. Plan seminars and other means by which teaching experience and professional content can be brought together.

In developing the laboratory phase of the curriculum, the staff followed the principle that the intern begins the Program by doing a limited amount of teaching with maximum assistance. Then, as he progresses through the Program, his teaching load is gradually increased while assistance given him is gradually decreased. The ways in which this principle has been implemented will be described later in this chapter.

It was obvious from the beginning of the Program in 1956 that the compartmentalization of professional content into courses was not the best way to structure this phase of the curriculum. Each day in his teaching the intern may be faced with problems which bear in some way on the commonly taught "foundation" courses in teacher education. For example, of what use in solving today's problems is a course in educational psychology which will not be given until the next semester? If professional content could be made meaningful by the intern's teaching experience, and if his teaching experience could be illuminated by the study of appropriate professional content, it was obvious to the staff that they must be experienced together in their use.

The need to direct curriculum content at a moving target complicated the problem of developing a Program curriculum. The intern teacher in his seventh week of summer teaching is hardly the same person he was in the first week. His growth has been marked, and his professional diet must change constantly to keep pace with that growth. During the first week he will need a little traditional content, drawn from several of the foundation subjects of teacher education; but by the seventh week he needs a more solid professional diet. Particular content can come too early or too late; it can be too much or too little.

A "spiral curiculum" was developed by the staff as the best way to construct an internship program of teacher education. This curriculum approach was particularly suited to the introduction of professional content concurrently with teaching experience. It met the criterion that this content be of the kind needed, be in the right amount, and be introduced at the proper time.

What is a spiral curriculum? Imagine a wheel (fig. 2) whose hub is the seminar topic, "planning." This theme was selected because it bears

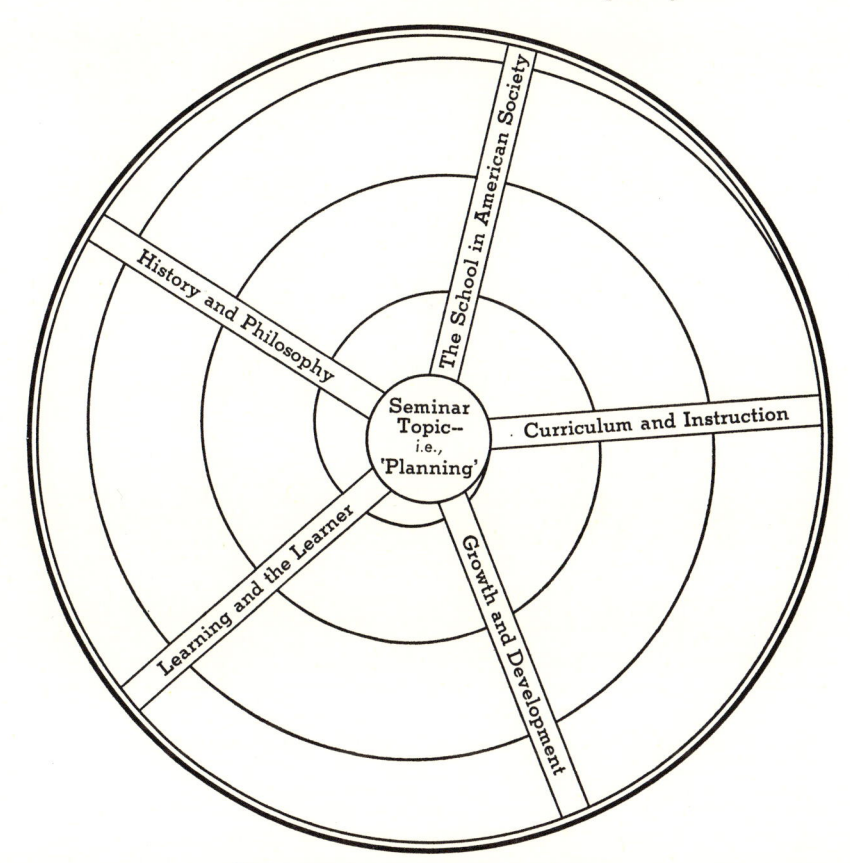

Fig. 2. The "spiral curriculum" concept.

on the problems which interns are immediately facing in the classroom. Broadly interpreted, planning involves all the elements in the teaching-learning situation. The spokes of the wheel are the content areas of teacher education. The curriculum begins near the hub and continues around it in ever-expanding spirals. As each spoke is crossed, information of the kind and in the amount needed is drawn from the content areas and included in the seminar.

How does the spiral curriculum operate? During the interns' first few days of teaching, a 360° swing around the hub, "planning," may be made in a single seminar, with all five of the spokes contributing content to the seminar topic for the day. Other seminar topics follow, such as "implementing instruction" and "evaluating instruction." Complete revolutions daily may soon give way to partial revolutions as the interns are ready for the study of a topic in greater depth. Eventually, the subject content represented by a single spoke ("Learning and the Learner," "Growth and Development," "Curriculum and Instruction," "The School in American Society," or "History and Philosophy") may contribute content for several consecutive seminars. In this way use of the spiral curriculum enabled the staff to guide interns to professional content beyond their immediate concerns but important to their continued growth in professional competence.

How was the spiral curriculum developed for use in the Graduate Internship Program in Teacher Education? The nature and scope of the curiculum-development problems faced by the staff are apparent when the elements shown in figures 1 and 2 of this chapter are combined in a single chart. Figure 3 places these elements in their chronological relationship. The problem of developing the curriculum was seen to involve:

1. The planning for and provision of suitable teaching and teaching-related experiences for interns.

2. The selection and organization of professional content of the kind and in the amount needed.

3. The provision of a seminar plan and schedule which makes possible the most effective integration of theory and practice.

4. The determination of seminar subjects and the selection of appropriate subject content for each.

5. The choice of the most effective ways of conducting the seminars.

6. The distribution of responsibilities for the seminars among members of the staff.

7. The constant evaluation of the curriculum and its elements as a basis for improvement.

This was the range of activities needed to design and manage a curriculum defined as including "all the learning experiences provided by the Program to prepare its members as teachers"! Obviously, the process is complex and was not accomplished easily; nor, for that matter is it easily described. Perhaps the best way to present the Graduate Internship curriculum is to depict the main types of learning experiences which have been and continue to be provided for interns in the Program.

PLANNED PRE-PROGRAM EXPERIENCES

Although the Program officially begins each year in June with the pre-internship summer of teaching, the intern's induction to his new vocation has already begun through those things learned in screening, selection, orientation, and placement activities.

The selection process described in chapter ii not only screens but also teaches. It focuses the attention of successful candidates on significant aspects of teaching. The transcript evaluation stresses the importance of academic preparation. In the group interview, the intern shares his thinking on public school education with others having similar interests and thereby gains new insights. The two personal interviews with staff members advance his readiness for the Program to follow.

Probably no pre-Program experiences further a candidate's under-

PROFESSIONAL CONTENT

1. Learning and the Learner
2. School in American Society
3. Growth and Development
4. History and Philosophy
5. Curriculum and Instruction

SEMINAR — Seminar Topic — SEMINAR

Pre-Program Experiences · Pre-Internship Summer · Internship Year · Post-Internship Summer

PLANNED EXPERIENCES

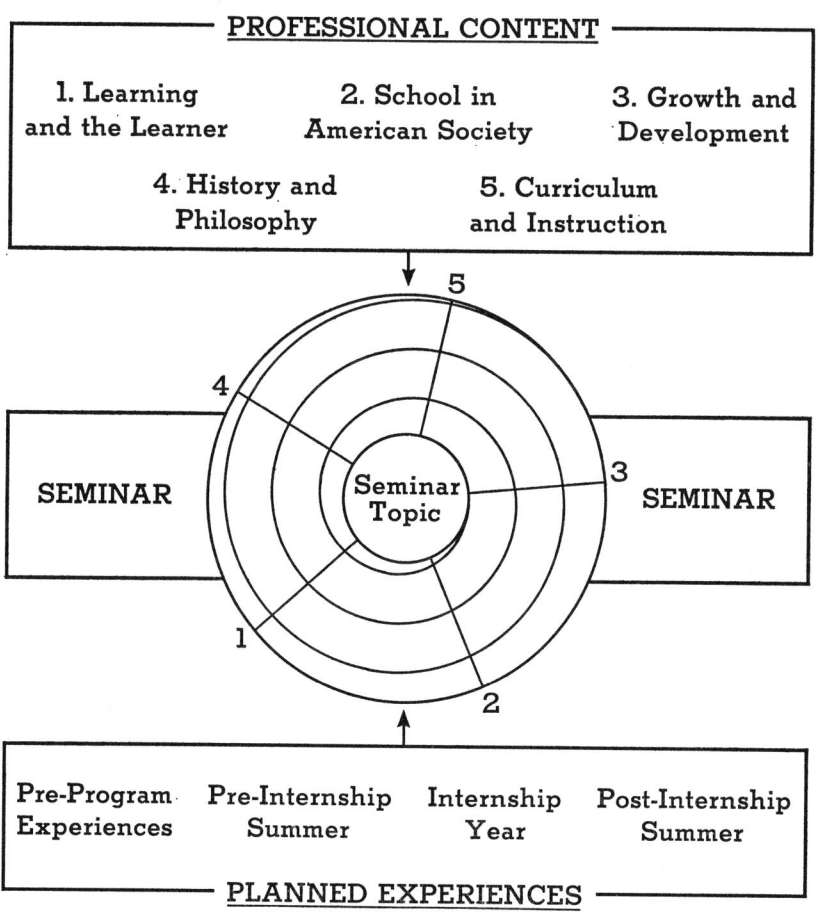

Fig. 3. The spiral curriculum.

standing of public school teaching more than his placement activities. Motivation could hardly be greater! First, he hears of the realities of job-hunting at the two placement-orientation meetings. Then he attends from one to four pre-placement meetings where public school administrators and intern candidates get together. More concentrated sessions of educational shop talk would be hard to imagine. Following these meetings he may be interviewed in one or more districts, where he can talk to department heads and teachers, visit classrooms, and read handbooks or other descriptive literature about the district, and even its courses of study. Ultimately, he will become knowledgeable about district policies, salary schedules, assignments, work loads, district expectations, and a teacher's responsibilities and opportunities.

After the intern finds employment for the coming school year, he is requested to arrange a visit to the school in which he will teach, for there is much to be learned about the school and his assignment. On this visit he is usually given a red-carpet welcome as a new member of the faculty. On a form provided by the Program he is to record such information as his teaching assignment, extra class responsibilities, audio-visual equipment available, the name of the school supervisor of beginning teachers, the department head or other person to whom an intern may go for assistance in his subject field, and school services of concern to the intern. He is asked to secure courses of study, basic texts, the teachers' handbook, the students' handbook, and any other materials which will be useful to him in preparing to teach in the fall. While the information and materials he obtains will be intrinsically valuable to him in his program of preparation, securing them makes him a better observer of the school in operation and helps him understand the profession he is preparing to enter.

During these pre-Program activities, group rapport can be seen in its early stages of development. The intern is happy when notified that he has been approved for membership and is proud to be one of such a select group. He finds that staff members are friendly, helpful, and sincerely concerned with him as an individual. The Program makes sense to him, and he finds in his placement activities that it has a good reputation in coöperating public schools. His forebodings tend to fade away, his enthusiasm grows, and he aspires to convert his potential as a teacher into the realities of successful classroom teaching.

In terms of his readiness to teach, the intern by June is hardly the same person who several months earlier submitted his application for membership in the Program. His professional preparation for teaching is already underway as he now enters the formal curriculum of teacher education.

THE PRE-INTERNSHIP SUMMER

The basic structure of the Graduate Internship Program was outlined in chapter i, pages 7–8. Pages 8–9 show the division of the 15-month Program into three parts—the pre-internship summer, the internship year of teaching, and the post-internship summer which complete the Program and qualify the intern for the California general secondary credential.

In order to provide suitable summer teaching assignments for 75 interns, two centers are now used, one at the Demonstration Secondary School operated by the University at Technical High School in Oakland and the other at Berkeley High in the Berkeley city school system. The summer curriculum of the Program is centered in these two schools, with interns and a six-member staff divided evenly between them. The program in each center is the same except for minor differences resulting from variations in school organization.

What is the intern's day throughout the first summer? It is long and strenuous. The intern reports at 7:45 A.M. and is busy until 3:30 P.M., five days a week for the seven weeks of summer school. Even when he leaves the building there is homework to be done: lessons must be planned and papers corrected. Then there are all the other jobs which teachers must do to get ready for the next day's teaching. How time-consuming those are for the enthusiastic, conscientious intern who wants so much to be successful! Sixteen-hour work days are not at all uncommon.

The school schedule provides for three 105-minute teaching periods in the morning and a common free period for all teachers after lunch when the pupils have gone home. Interns teach one of these morning periods. During another period they participate in a small-group seminar composed of 12 to 13 with a staff member in charge. A third morning period, for use as the intern sees fit, provides time for a variety of activities such as observation of other classes, conferences with staff members or master teachers,[1] work with audio-visual equipment, special interest movies, study in the library, or preparation for the next teaching period. The afternoon period when the pupils have gone is used by the interns for work with the master teachers. Finally, when the day is over for the master teachers, (2 P.M.) the interns attend a large-

---

[1] The teachers who are employed as regular members of the summer high school faculty will be referred to as "master teachers."

group seminar in which the more formal professional content is presented. By the end, it has been a long and busy day for the intern.

Teaching Experience

Realistic teaching experience is the heart of the intern's activities even during this initial summer period. The intern begins teaching after the briefest possible period of observation and participation. To speed up his induction period each intern is assigned before summer school begins to a master teacher of the subject which the intern will be teaching in the fall. In preparation for the summer session these two persons get acquainted in order to plan the course they will teach, to assemble materials, to prepare their room, and to consider ways they can work together most effectively. Often a close friendship and feelings of mutual confidence develop quickly.

Thus by the time school opens the intern has had several busy days of "getting ready." Over a period of time staff members have conveyed to him a feeling of their confidence in his ability to teach. The master teacher is supportive, recognizing the intern's strong subject-matter background and his eagerness for help in learning how to teach. "Interns before me have plunged into teaching and survived," the intern thinks, "Why can't I?" Pupils, as they appear in class the first day of school, find that they have not one, but two teachers. From the start, the intern begins to feel and act like a full-fledged teacher, and amazingly soon he begins to fit his new role.

In general, it is recommended that the intern work in a subordinate role at first, delaying the assumption of extensive teaching responsibilities for a few days to permit him to observe the master teacher. Then there follows a gradual increase in teaching involvement. However, it has not been found advisable to set rigid policies controlling the manner and timing of the intern's induction into teaching, since Program experience has indicated that there is *no single best way*. Individual differences among interns and among master teachers make it advisable to permit each "teaching team" to develop a plan which is best for them. There are interns who do some teaching the first day of school; others do no teaching for several days. Usually by the end of the first week, some have assumed the major teaching responsibility, and generally all have begun teaching for at least part of the class period.

There are several reasons for this early involvement. Each intern teacher should find his own style of teaching and develop his own supporting philosophy. To prevent the natural tendency merely to imitate more experienced models and to insure the intern's own growth and understanding of his identity in the classroom, the Graduate Internship Program wants interns in front of the class as soon as possible. It never wants them to feel that there is only a single *right way* to teach. One intern's log includes this comment:

> As I was plunged into teaching the very first day of summer school without even having had the opportunity to watch a high school teacher practice his art, I was struck by one single thought: "How am I going to start? What am I going to tell them?" Even though I felt pretty confident in the subject I was assigned to teach, I had a strong feeling of inadequacy in methods. To my surprise I found something to say and I proceeded to talk to the class in French, using simple words, about the beauty of Paris. Apparently they were delighted and two students came to me after class to tell me, "We have never had anything like this!"

When the intern does begin to teach, his first teaching experience comes through presenting an instructional unit which he has helped plan and which he is prepared to teach. From the beginning, the intern must realize that teaching involves both planning before class and the execution of these plans in the classroom. Both phases must be seen as interdependent elements of effective teaching. When plans for a lesson to be taught by an intern are prepared by a master teacher, one part of the teaching experience is diminished. Furthermore, few persons can execute another's plans effectively. One intern's experience illustrates this point. Thrust into a poetry unit already begun and pre-structured by his master teacher, he was unable to teach it, so anxious was he to carry through his master teacher's intentions. A staff member suggested that he withdraw temporarily and prepare his own unit. When he returned to the classroom a few days later with his own material, he was entirely in command and very effective.

It is important not only that interns think of themselves as teachers, but that they be respected by the pupils as teachers rather than as students learning to teach. Only through full assumption of the teaching can interns be fully effective and gain the most from their summer experience. One intern expressed her conviction as follows:

> Fortunately my master teacher gave me the class the first day, and it has been mine ever since. My first response to this idea was negative. However, I see the value of it now and am happy that it was handled this way. The students know me as their teacher and not as a person who takes charge of the class only for testing and routine purposes.

Although there is much profit in observing master teachers and in reading professional literature, the "feel" of teaching can be had only through the act itself. When the intern is before a class he realizes the enormous gap between knowing a subject and knowing how to arouse appreciation of it; between an intellectual understanding of adolescents and the ability to inspire and guide a restless group of 30 boys and girls in the classroom. He begins to see the difference between pumping knowledge *in* and drawing understanding *out* of the student. Firsthand experience with adolescents—gazing vacantly out the windows, noisy, and shuffling in their seats, smirking and unmotivated, confused and even belligerent—confronts the intern with the realities of teaching. This comment from an intern's evaluation of the first week is typical:

The idea that practical experience is the best teacher of teachers was one that was of primary importance to me when I entered the Internship Program. I have always found it difficult to learn any job or type of work until I actually encountered it. From my experiences in the classroom this last week I have gained much more than I could have gleaned from texts or other less immediate sources.

If the metaphor which identifies the teaching experiences of interns as the heart of the Graduate Internship Program curriculum has merit, then it follows that this heart must be thoroughly sound if the organism is to live. Only when the intern begins teaching do all the other learning experiences which make up his curriculum really begin to pulsate with life.

Supportive Supervision

"Sink or swim" is not the attitude of the master teacher or the Program staff as the intern plunges into teaching the first summer. All the resources of the Program support him. Each staff member is responsible for the supervision of 12 or 13 interns, and, knowing that beginning days in teaching are critical, he works closely with master teachers and interns. He is never far away, ready to give needed help at a moment's notice.

It is at this time that the mutual feelings of friendship and confidence developed between staff members and interns during screening and placement activities begin to pay big dividends. When there is a basis of friendship, supervision can be truly supportive. Channels of communication are open. The intern reveals rather than conceals his concerns, and his own perceptions of his problems provide the basis for assistance.

The intern realizes that no one expects him to have reached the mythical state of perfection in so complicated a task as the instruction of the young. He knows that some mistakes are expected and can be the basis of valuable learning, so he tends to mention his mistakes to his supervisor as freely as his successes. By helping him analyze his difficulties and the reasons for his failure or success, the supervisor helps him derive the greatest benefit from his teaching.

The staff supervisor finds numerous ways to assist the intern. It may be in the planning of an instructional unit or in the teaching itself. Help may be sought on problems of classroom management. During the first few critical days of teaching the staff supervisor is sometimes of greatest assistance when merely bolstering the intern's confidence. The time, duration, and number of visits to the classroom vary widely according to the particular personality characteristics of the intern and the nature of the problems he faces. In much of the assistance given, classroom visitation is not required. With very few exceptions, interns welcome a visit by their staff supervisor and commonly request him to come by. They ask him to see a class which is presenting problems as often as they ask him to observe one which is going well.

Seminars

Early in the chapter the curriculum was defined as "all the learnings provided by the Program to prepare its members as teachers." These learnings, it was pointed out, come from classroom experiences planned for interns (practice) and from professional content (theory), with the seminar serving to integrate practice and theory (figure 1, page 37). The use of a spiral curriculum has facilitated this integration. The teaching experiences of interns during the pre-internship summer have been described. The professional content of the curriculum and its determination will now be considered in relation to the Program seminars.

The process by which the staff determines the professional content of seminars consists of three steps:

Step 1. The selection and storage of appropriate content.—From the body of professional content generally considered to provide the foundations for teacher education, the staff has selected and organized the content thought to be most helpful to beginning teachers. In these five curriculum warehouses it stockpiles strategic materials—

Learning and the learner
The school in American society
Growth and development of the adolescent
Secondary school curriculum and instruction
History and philosophy of Education.

Selected bibliographies are prepared for each content area, key studies are identified, and useful materials are located or assembled. In a sense, the five outlines are the Program's course of study. But this selected and stored professional content is not the Program curriculum; as it exists, it is not suited to the daily needs of interns.

Step 2. Determination of current intern needs.—The staff must now look to the classroom where the interns are teaching and growing in competence. What are their general problems? What topics should be considered in the daily seminars to help interns grow? From experience with successive groups of interns, staff members can anticipate with some accuracy the nature of their changing needs. From close working relationships with the current group, they can sense minor deviations from the normal growth pattern. With this knowledge, they can determine an appropriate sequence of seminar topics for the immediate future.

Step 3. Planning seminars.—A specific seminar will be used to illustrate how steps 1 and 2 are the basis of seminar planning.

In keeping with plans developed well before the opening of summer school, seminars during the first week of the summer focus on planning for teaching, with special attention given to the ways in which the teacher organizes the various elements making up the teaching-learning situation in the classroom. "Classroom management" is the seminar topic on Tuesday (step 2, above) and the staff is planning the presentation. What content should be included? In seeking an answer to this question, they turn their attention to the selected and stored content (step 1, above). It is obvious that each of the five areas includes information which will help interns with their problems of management. The staff now decides, in general, what will be drawn from each stockpile, in what amounts, how it will be organized under a single topic, the manner in which it will be presented, and the staff member or members who will be responsible for the seminars. Following this general plan, they make the detailed preparations and conduct the seminar.

A little information from each of several pertinent content areas is all that interns can use now; more would be too much. But a week later "discipline" may be the seminar topic. Content from the same professional areas is presented, but now it can be of greater breadth and depth, expanding previously acquired concepts and adding others. In a week or two, an entire seminar profitably may be devoted to a consideration of "motivation" and to "discipline"—each an element of classroom management. In these three seminars is there an overlapping of subject content? Certainly, just as there is an overlapping in the problems an intern faces during his first, second, and third weeks of teaching!

Successive seminars planned in this way are the basis of the spiral curriculum described earlier in this chapter. They are the means by which appropriate professional content and present teaching experience are interrelated so that each makes its maximum contribution to the professional growth of intern teachers.

Seminars are of two types—"large group" and "small group." During the summer the large group includes the 37-38 interns teaching in a center, and during the internship year it includes the total group of 75 interns meeting on the campus. Throughout the Program, the small group is composed of 12-13 interns. The large-group seminars tend to be content-oriented; the small-group seminars experience-oriented. However, there is a constant convergence of theory and practice in both.

1. *The Small-Group Seminar.*—Unlike peas in a pod, the interns in a small group form, by design, a heterogeneous group. First, an attempt is made to have one or more representatives from each subject field in the small group. Then a balance is sought within and between groups by giving recognition to such factors as age, sex, vocational background, personality characteristics, and special interests and aptitudes. Just putting such a diverse group of individuals in close contact from day to day provides considerable stimulation to all—they "spark" each other. While they differ, one from another, interns have the common purpose to become good teachers. They develop an *esprit de corps* difficult to describe, but impressive to observe. The knowledge that they are together in a profession new to them seems to nuture their coöperative impulses and strengthen their friendships.

Since the staff leader of the seminar supervises the teaching of all members of his group, he is able to identify their current common problems and needs. He can direct discussions accordingly and feed in ideas and materials at strategic moments. He can know when to allay anxieties, when to reassure interns about their present performance, and when to let them know that they are ready to raise their standards and increase their demands upon themselves. Without detracting from the spontaneity of the group, the staff leader works to make each seminar meeting of maximum value to all its members.

The sharing of anxieties about teaching helps the intern overcome them. The first teaching experience is usually traumatic for anyone—including an intern. Shocked into an awareness of the challenge of teaching, the new teacher often needs to avoid disappointments. Knowing others are being similarly confronted and dismayed helps him place his own difficulties in perspective. An intern who was one of the first persons to begin teaching in the summer of 1961 made the following report to her seminar. Imagine how reassuring her experience was to others.

> I was petrified and wanted to run out of the room when the master teacher turned the class over to me. I hadn't been expecting it and I was sure I would fall on my face. But before I knew it, I heard myself talking about the assigned essay and behaving as a teacher. When I saw the students' hands go up in response to a question, I knew I was in business.

As others in the group had their first teaching experience, they, too, gave reassuring reports and soon everyone in the group was eager to find out how well he would respond to the challenge of the next few days. Relieved of the enervating burden of self-doubt, interns can begin to focus on the important aspects of the teaching-learning process in the classroom.

One intern appraised the small group seminar in these words:

> I feel that in many ways this is the most vital and helpful part of the entire program. It is here that the impressions of the large group seminar talks are sorted, sifted, and analyzed. It is here that we can discuss our problems, our conflicting philosophies, our successes and failures in teaching, and anything else that bears directly or indirectly on our experiences in the Program. While we also do this to a certain extent with our master teachers and our colleagues in our own subject area, these discussions are more likely to be hasty and intermittent, carried on in the cafeteria over the hubbub and the many distractions which inevitably occur. The atmosphere in our seminar group is, on the other hand, relaxed, leisurely, and much quieter.
>
> I think, too, that our leader is excellent. He provides, in an unobtrusive way, just enough direction to keep the discussion from degenerating into a free-for-all or collapsing under its own weight; but not enough to prevent us from exploring creatively the many issues which come up....

The teaching experience of interns, obviously, can provide only a part of the seminar content. In addition, content must be drawn from the field of Education and supporting disciplines and injected judiciously into the seminar. This is a responsibility of the staff coördinator, who may provide such content himself or direct the interns to other sources. However, it is the large-group seminar which bears major responsibility for acquainting the intern with this professional content.

2. *Large-Group Seminar.*—Late in the afternoon, when pupils are gone, master teachers have completed their day, and the building is quiet, interns meet in the large-group seminar. These meetings may

involve members of the staff, a guest speaker, master teachers and administrators in the summer school, former interns, and sometimes current interns. Films which supplement curriculum content are shown occasionally. When appropriate, discussion groups are formed after the general meetings, or issues which develop are carried over into the discussions of the small groups the following day.

The large-group seminar is used to present organized professional content as opposed to the content of the small-group seminar. Content for the large-group seminar can be planned to supplement their experiences; content for the small-group seminar emerges from their teaching experiences. A balance between the two is needed, for too great emphasis on the first may ignore the daily teaching needs of interns as too great emphasis on the second may ignore long-term needs and leave unfortunate gaps in the teacher's professional preparation.

"Although I never worked so hard, I enjoyed the summer." This comment reflects a frequently expressed attitude of interns as they viewed in retrospect their first summer. Year after year staff members are unprepared for the professional growth they have observed in particular interns and in the group as a whole. This rapid blossoming of teaching skills in seven weeks seems no less spectacular than the blossoming of a flower when shown by time-lapse photography.

INTERNSHIP YEAR

With their summer of preparation completed, the Program teachers are ready for their internship year of teaching, the second phase of the Graduate Internship Program. Now they have a dual responsibility— to the Program and to the school district. Intern teachers must perform to the satisfaction of both of these agencies. Obviously, a close working relationship between coöperating schools and the Graduate Internship Program is essential and it has existed throughout the life of the Program. Since good teaching is the common goal, they work together to further the intern teachers' professional growth.

Classroom teaching experience, supervision, and seminars, the basic elements of the summer curriculum, remain basic elements during the internship year. Now a full day of teaching replaces the single-period teaching responsibility of the summer. Now University supervision is supplemented by the regular supervisory services of the school, rather than by the supervision of the master teacher. Now three-hour Saturday morning seminars held on the campus every other week replace the daily seminars of the summer. Teaching, supervision and seminars continue to influence the professional growth of interns as they did during the summer program: however, these elements are newly structured to fit the changed setting of the internship year.

Internship Teaching

The intern has a dual role during his internship year of teaching. He is concurrently a teaching member of a school faculty and a student member of a teacher education program. The relative importance given these two roles by the intern and by others affect his conduct and professional growth in subtle but significant ways. When one of his two roles is conceived as an "end," the other becomes a "means." For example, if successful teaching is the end to be attained, then supporting program activities become the means by which this on-the-job effectiveness is attained. But, if the successful completion of a credential program is the end, then his teaching is seen merely as the means by which the program is completed. In the Graduate Internship Program the intern's role as a student member of a teacher education program is always subordinated to his role as a teaching member of a school faculty.

The characteristics of a particular teacher education program influence the role of its members. For example, the student teacher in traditional programs does not have and can not feel that he has equal status with regular teachers. They *teach;* he is a *practice teacher.* The intern, on the other hand, is and can feel that he is a regular member of the school faculty, although only a beginner. As he starts his teaching in the fall, his professional identification shifts from the Graduate Internship Program to his school. Only as this "weaning" takes place is the intern ready to make his maximum contribution to the district and achieve maximum professional growth for himself. Many elements in the structure and procedures of the Program help the intern see himself as a regular teacher.

Nothing is done to set the intern apart from other beginning teachers when he is assigned to his school. He is a full-time teacher and is completely responsible for the classes he teaches and for extra-class assignments which may be given him. His commitments to the Program do not interfere in any way with his primary obligations to the school in which he teaches. He has been placed on the regular salary schedule of the district according to his academic preparation and is paid in the same way as other teachers.

If members of the school faculty know that the intern is enrolled in the Graduate Internship Program and is in the process of completing requirements for a general secondary credential, it is usually because they have been given this information by the intern himself. Most interns make no point of either hiding or disclosing their unique status because the distinction now seems pointless—it has no real or imagined negative connotations. Some interns freely explain their status because they feel that the Program has a good reputation and they are proud of their membership in it.

No single feature of the Program does more to establish the primacy of the interns' role as a member of a school faculty than his commitment to teach at least two years where he is initially employed. When a district offers an intern candidate a contract, it does so with the expectation that he will succeed and remain a member of the teaching staff. When the intern accepts a contract, he does so knowing that he is choosing the school in which he will begin his new career and, hopefully, where he will be wanted and will want to remain.

It is important that the intern perceive himself to be *a teacher who is learning,* rather than *a learner who is teaching.* The Graduate Internship Program stresses the former role, for once established it need never be changed. The good teacher must always remain a student.

Supervision

Intern teachers are supervised throughout the school year by University personnel. Five or six supervisors of particular subject matter fields from the regular secondary Teacher Education staff provide assistance in their respective subject fields. The six Graduate Internship Program staff members provide more general supervision, usually for the same interns they worked with in the summer session. In addition to providing adequate supervisory personnel, this coöperative arrangement assures the availability of a supervisor with special competence in each intern's teaching field. The assisting supervisors meet each month with Program staff members to plan and coördinate their activities. In addition, each GIP staff member works informally, as needed, with those persons who are supervising intern members of his small group in order to exchange helpful information.

The intern is encouraged to request help and not to depend wholly upon the school visits of his supervisor. Consequently, much assistance received by the intern is not the result of classroom observation, but may be accomplished through phone calls, conferences on the campus, or even special meetings, when a supervisor brings a number of his interns together at his home for consideration of their individual and common problems. No attempt is made to place school visitations on a rigid schedule, but rather to let their frequency and duration be determined by the needs of each intern teacher. On the average, however, a supervisor sees an intern in his school about every other week.

Since the intern is both an employee of a school district and a member of the Graduate Internship Program, the University supervisor must coördinate his activities with the supervisory activities of the district. This requires an understanding of its curriculum, policies, and procedures, and the ability to operate tactfully but effectively with supervisors and administrators of the school. A classroom visit is of little value unless the supervisor and the intern teacher are able to confer following the observation. With the intern carrying a full teaching load, conferences must be held during his free period, the lunch period, or after school. Often interns and supervisors meet on the campus when extended conference time is required.

Seminars

On alternate Saturday mornings from nine o'clock until noon throughout the school year, interns attend seminars on the campus conducted by members of the Program staff. As during the summer, the large-group and small-group seminars are the basic instructional units. The former draws heavily upon a structured body of professional content and the latter upon the teaching experiences of the interns. As in the summer seminar program, theory and practice are integrated through the use of the spiral curriculum. Occasionally, too, interns meet in subject groups to consider matters of specific concern in their teaching fields.

Staff members share the responsibility for the large-group seminars, and each member directs the activities of a small-group seminar of 12–13 interns, including those he supervises. A typical morning is divided between the two seminar types, with some time usually given by the small group to a discussion of the content presented in the large group. Guest speakers are used occasionally. When a particularly outstanding speaker is scheduled, externs are invited to attend and participate.

Post-Internship Summer

In completing the Program during the second summer, the intern must satisfy two requirements. If he does not have six post-graduate units in his teaching field, he must take them to satisfy present credential requirements of the State of California. Finally, all members of the intern group return to the campus early in August for a four-week workshop in educational psychology. The eight units earned in the pre-internship summer, the ten units earned during the internship year, and the six academic units and four professional units earned in the post-internship summer complete a 28-unit credential program, 22 of which are professional. The intern thus completes the Graduate Internship Program and qualifies for a California general secondary credential which replaces the internship-type credential on which he has been teaching.

Some interns met the academic six-unit post-graduate requirement upon entry into the Program and attend only the four-week workshop. Those who have not met the academic requirement previously must secure Program approval of the courses they plan to take during the summer.

Each summer, for a short period early in August, there are 150 interns in the Program—a group of 75 beginning their work and 75 completing their work. Since the full time of all regular staff members must be spent with the new group, an educational psychologist is employed as an instructor for those completing the Program. This group meets each morning from nine o'clock to twelve, with afternoon hours available for conferences, work in the library, and special meetings.

The course in educational psychology presents an organized body of content and requires each intern to do extensive work in an area of particular concern to him. Since all interns have had a year of teaching, they are able to relate psychological concepts to their recent experience with students in the classroom. Having been alerted to the requirements of the summer workshop, many of them begin in the spring to gather data for their special project and to collect materials which will be useful. Thus, the culminating summer activities tend to be related to their teaching experience as are previous elements of the Program curriculum.

Problems in Curriculum Development

Another full account of curriculum development in the Graduate Internship Program might be written for the purpose of explaining what the staff did to achieve, maintain, or regain the balance needed among elements of the curriculum. Like a complicated machine, an alteration in one operating part may throw other parts out of adjustment: in solving one curriculum problem, others may arise. What professional content should be presented? In what amount? When is the right time? How should it be presented? By whom? Such questions as these concerned the staff throughout the Program. The right answer was not easy to determine because so many interdependent factors were involved in every decision. Ignore one factor or give another too great an emphasis, and the needed balance is lost—the effectiveness of the curriculum is reduced.

A few examples will illustrate the problems of balance which the staff faced. When curriculum content depended too much on the interns' teaching experience, there was a tendency toward dilution, omission, and fragmentation of professional content; but when there was too much dependence on the organized body of content, seminars were less meaningful and interns tended to be disinterested. When interns in their first days of summer teaching are concerned with survival in the classroom, attempts to introduce such seminar topics as, "The Secondary School in America," proved discouraging. Failure to assess the "common denominator" at a particular time in the concerns of intern group members resulted in seminars of value only to a limited number. The assumption that a seminar which was effective last year would, without change, be equally effective the next year proved false and demonstrated that there were significant differences between groups from year to year. With so many factors such as these to be considered, seminar planning was found to be a balancing act.

"Why wasn't this thought of and tried before?" This question often was asked by members of the staff as a curriculum addition or modification strengthened the Program. The manner in which the small-group seminar belatedly became a part of the pre-internship summer program illustrates this point. The small-group seminar did not appear until the third year of the Program; but it quickly was recognized as indispensable. For the first two years, interns had a second teaching assignment during the school period in which they now attend this daily seminar. If one teaching period is good, two periods would be better—this was the original reasoning. Experience with this teaching schedule during the first two years raised doubts regarding the validity of the assumption. Another problem was of concern to the staff during these first two years. Efforts to make the large-group seminar the vehicle for the presentation of an organized body of professional content were often frustrated by the injection of interns' "nuts and bolts" concerns growing out of their teaching experiences. This problem and the problems growing out of the two-period teaching assignment were solved through a single change—the introduction of the small-group seminar, in place of the second teaching assignment. While this program change has been by far the most significant single improvement in the curriculum, others have come about in a similar manner.

In an experience-oriented curriculum, there is always the possibility that elements of the organized body of professional subject matter will not be considered and there will be "blind spots" in the teacher's preparation. Two factors minimize this possibility in the Program. First, when seminars are related to the interns' teaching experiences throughout their summer of part-time teaching and their internship year of full-time teaching, consideration will probably be given to all the professional content usually included in teacher education programs. Second, to guard against possible omissions, the staff periodically takes an inventory of the professional content in its five warehouses. What has been withdrawn? At what time in the Program? In what amounts? Should unused content be injected at some point into the curriculum, or should it be eliminated? As the staff constantly asks and answers such questions as these in relation to the professional growth of interns, curriculum development becomes a continuous process.

CHAPTER V

THE INTERN AS A PUBLIC SCHOOL EMPLOYEE

Up to this point, we have depicted the characteristics of interns as they entered the Program (chapter iii), and have outlined the professional curriculum to which they were subjected (chapter iv). We now turn to a examination of interns as school district employees during their year of internship teaching. Where have they taught, what have they taught, whom have they taught, and with what success?

THE EMPLOYING DISTRICTS AND SCHOOLS

Number

Section VI of the California Association of School Administrators, representing school districts within reasonable geographic radius of the University, coöperated in initiating the Graduate Internship Teacher Education Program. In the pilot (1956) group, 11 of these districts participated in the Program with Oakland being the principal employer of interns, hiring 8 of the 23. In the second year, 1957, the number of districts providing places of employment for interns grew to 25, with Oakland again the principal partner, employing 15 interns. Since that time the number of school districts having interns in a single year has increased to 31 in 1961. Oakland has employed 55 interns—a total equal to that of all the interns hired by all districts in 1957, the second year the Program was in operation.

Of the 46 different districts employing interns during the six-year period (table 18), five employed interns each of the six years; eight districts employed interns each of four years; another eight districts, each of three years. The continuity of the initial employment of interns by the same districts signifies a positive attitude of administrative staffs toward the Program and implies recognition of the excellent teachers which interns become.

Schools

During the six-year period, the 333 interns have been assigned to teach in 124 different schools in the 46 participating districts. The names of the schools, the grade level of the school, and the number assigned are shown in tables A-1 and A-2 in the Appendix. At two high schools one or more interns has been placed for each of the six years; at two other high schools interns have been placed for each of five years; and at ten schools interns have been placed for each of four years.

TABLE 18
Assignment of Interns to School Districts[a]

School districts	\multicolumn{6}{c}{Number of interns assigned each year}	Total number of interns	Number of years of district's participation in the program	Total number of district schools to which interns were assigned
	1956	1957	1958	1959	1960	1961			
Acalanes	..	1	..	..	3	..	4	2	3
Alameda	1	1	3	1	3	1	10	6	2
Albany	1	..	..	1	2	..	4	3	1
Alhambra	..	1	1	..	..	1	3	3	1
Amador	1	..	2	1	..	1	5	4	1
Antioch	1	1	1	1	2	..	6	5	2
Berkeley	2	5	3	8	3	5	26	6	2
Campbell	..	..	..	..	..	2	2	1	2
Carquinez	..	1	..	1	1	..	3	3	1
Castro Valley	..	1	2	2	..	1	6	4	2
Contra Costa	..	..	1	..	..	1	2	2	1
Hayward High	3	4	4	4	7	3	25	6	7
Hayward Elem	..	1	..	..	..	..	1	1	1
Irvington	..	..	..	..	..	1	1	1	1
Jefferson	..	..	..	..	..	1	1	1	1
Lafayette	..	1	1	1	1	1	5	5	1
Liberty	..	1	..	..	..	..	1	1	1
Livermore	..	..	1	1	..	3	5	3	1
Mt. Diablo	..	3	4	4	4	4	19	5	7
Mt. Eden	..	..	..	..	1	1	2	2	1
Mtn. View	..	..	1	..	..	2	3	2	2
Napa	..	..	..	..	..	3	3	1	2
Novato	..	..	..	..	1	1	2	2	1
Oakland	8	15	9	10	6	7	55	6	20
Palo Alto	..	..	2	2	1	..	5	3	3
Petaluma	..	..	..	..	1	1	2	2	2
Piedmont	1	..	2	..	1	..	4	3	1
Pinole-Hercules	..	..	..	..	..	1	1	1	1
Pittsburg	..	..	2	1	3	..	6	3	3
Redwood City	..	1	..	..	..	..	1	1	1
Richmond	1	3	3	2	1	2	12	6	6
Rio Vista	..	..	..	..	1	..	1	1	1
San Francisco	..	4	5	1	1	..	11	4	6
San Leandro	..	2	3	4	3	3	15	5	3
San Mateo Elem	..	1	2	1	2	..	6	4	3
San Mateo High	..	2	3	2	..	3	10	4	5
San Rafael	3	1	..	1	1	5	11	5	5
San Ramon	..	1	1	..	1	2	5	4	1
Sequoia	..	1	2	3	3	2	11	5	5
Sonoma	1	1	..	2	1	2	7	5	1
South S. F.	..	..	..	..	2	1	3	2	3
John Swett	..	..	..	..	2	1	3	2	1
Tamalpais	..	1	1	1	..	3	6	4	2
Vallejo	..	1	2	3	..	..	6	3	3
Walnut Creek	..	..	..	..	1	..	1	1	1
Washington	..	..	2	2	1	7	12	4	3
Total	23	55	63	60	60	72	333	..	124

[a] Interns were employed prior to June as a condition for acceptance into the Program.

In the year 1956 the ratio of interns initially employed in junior (or intermediate) and in senior (or four-year) high schools was 12 to 11. In the 1961 group it had shifted to from 17 to 55. These figures indicate a trend—a shift in the placement of interns from junior (or intermediate) schools to senior (or four-year) high schools. In all, interns were assigned to 69 senior (or four-year) high schools and to 52 junior high (or intermediate) schools.[1] This total of 121 schools leaves three schools unaccounted for in the total of 124 different schools enumerated in table 18. The discrepancy is explained by the fact that five interns were assigned to teach in grades 13 and 14 of a junior college. Two such assignments were made to Contra Costa College, one in 1959 and another in 1961; one to Oakland City College in 1957 and another in 1958; and one to San Francisco City College in 1958. In 1959, the University inaugurated a special junior college internship program to take care of the increasing demand for interns at this level.

Teaching Locations

In a number of the schools to which interns were assigned, there was a shortage of classrooms, in many cases necessitating maximum scheduling of their use. This in turn meant that a number of interns had to move from one classroom to another during their five-, six-, or seven-period teaching day, rather than remain in one room the whole day. The "traveling" teacher must carry with him, period by period, all the books, materials, aids, and other teaching paraphernalia he needs for each class. This is an extra burden for beginning teachers. Because it was a source of considerable complaint among interns in the 1956 and 1957 groups, the Program staff investigated this period-to-period traveling by the 1958 and 1959 groups.

In the two groups, there were 122 interns. The number of teaching locations for each is shown in table 19. For example, in the 1958 group, 35 of the 62 taught in the same classroom all day, eleven had two locations, and another eleven had three. Four interns traveled to four different classrooms during the day and one intern spent his entire six-period day rushing from one room to another.

As shown by table 19, there is little or no discernible difference in the two groups in the extent of room-to-room "travel." In one case 35 interns and in the other case 37 remained in the same location all day. In both groups five interns had four or more different locations during the day.

[1] Intermediate schools are seventh and eighth grade schools maintained by kindergarten-to-eighth-grade elementary school districts.

Obviously the 50 interns who were forced to travel one or more times faced not only the extra problems brought on by the sheer necessity of physically moving but also the psychological effects of having no permanent home within the school—no place to "hang their hats" or desks to call their own. First-year teaching is difficult at best and having to be a "pack rat" teacher adds unnecessary problems for

TABLE 19
NUMBER OF TEACHING LOCATIONS
(1958 and 1959 Groups)

Year	\multicolumn{6}{c	}{Number of teaching locations}	Number of interns
	1	2	3	4	5	6	
1958...............	35	11	11	4	0	1	62[a]
1959...............	37	11	7	3	2	0	60
Total.........	72	22	18	7	2	1	122

[a] In the data presented in chap. iii, the number 63 has been used since this was the number of interns who entered the program in June of 1958. During the 1958 summer session, one intern was dropped from the program; hence the data on teaching assignments were based on the 62 who taught in public schools during the 1958–1959 school year.

intern teachers. Certainly teaching with a wide variety of resources, materials, and devices was the kind expected of interns, and the conditions of travel doubtless served as a deterrent toward achievement of this end.

The significance of traveling to the measured effectiveness of teaching was not determined for these interns since the principal when rating their effectiveness was asked to give recognition to this and similar factors in the physical environment of the teacher's assignment (see Evaluation Form in Appendix). The specific effect of such factors on the success of beginning teachers merits further study.

UTILIZATION OF MAJOR–MINOR FIELDS OF PREPARATION

A resurgent concern for the teaching of subject matter in public schools has focused increased attention on the academic preparation of teachers. The extent of interns' preparation in subject matter has been discussed in chapter iii. As important as is this part of their preparation, equally important is it that teachers be assigned to teach in their fields of specialization. Without such an assignment, a teacher's strength in his collegiate major and minor concentration is largely wasted.

Because the staff of the Graduate Internship Teacher Education Program believes firmly that teachers must be well-grounded in the subjects they are to teach, they make every effort to effect individual assignments of interns in their major or minor fields. Final responsibility here, however, lies with the employing school district.

Optimum use of major-minor fields of academic preparation is assured when teachers teach only in their major and/or their minor

TABLE 20
UTILIZATION OF FIELDS OF PREPARATION OF INTERNS

Fields of assignment	Per cent						
	1956	1957	1958	1959	1960	1961	Over-all
Major field exclusively............	50	63	56	47	56	64	56
Minor field exclusively...........	6	7	11	14	12	17	11
Major and minor fields only......	11	7	8	12	12	10	10
Major and minor and others......	6	7	4	5	3	1	4
Major and others than minor.....	11	9	9	7	12	4	9
Minor and others than major.....	0	0	4	4	3	1	2
Neither major nor minor.........	16	7	8	11	2	3	8

fields. Partial utilization of such preparation occurs when *some* teaching is done in major and minor fields, but also in other subjects outside these areas. Minimum use is realized when they teach neither in their major nor in their minor. Utilization of the fields of preparation of the 333 interns is shown in table 20.

If one includes the major and minor field combinations, the data in table 20 reveal that 92 per cent of the interns were assigned to utilize their specialized academic preparation. Comparison of intern assignments with similar data about California secondary school teachers in general shows that, on the whole, interns fare no better than their conventionally prepared colleagues. Comparative data are shown in table 21.[2]

However, the coöperative nature of the Graduate Internship Teacher Education Program ought to have resulted in a closer meshing of teacher preparation with teacher assignment. Certainly this was the expectation of the Program staff. Consequently, in the fall of 1958, it was decided to take a closer look at this problem by studying the 1958 and 1959 groups.

[2] *California Teachers: Their Professional Qualifications, Experience, and the Size of Their Classes, 1956–1957.* Bulletin of the California State Department of Educaton, XXVII, No. 10 (Sacramento: October, 1956), 20.

In both groups, each intern kept a period-by-period record of his teaching assignment in the school including subject(s) and room assignment(s). From these records, the actual number of class-periods each intern taught in his major, in his minor, or in neither was determined. These total the number of class-periods taught by all interns in all subject fields.

TABLE 21

UTILIZATION OF FIELDS OF PREPARATION OF CALIFORNIA
SECONDARY SCHOOL TEACHERS 1946 AND 1956

	Per cent	
	1956	1946
Major field only	51.6	58.6
Minor field only	8.7	8.8
Major and minor fields only	13.8	10.4
Major and minor fields, plus other subjects	4.6	3.8
Major field and subjects other than minor field	11.7	8.7
Minor field and subjects other than major field	3.6	3.2
Neither major nor minor field	6.0	6.5

Teaching in the Major Field

For the two years studied (table 22), of 26 social science majors none taught six periods in their major fields, three taught five periods, two four periods, three three periods, one two periods, five one period, and twelve taught no periods at all. The total is 39 class-periods a day taught in the major field—social science in this case; but the total would have been 156 periods instead, had all those prepared in social sciences taught six periods a day in their area of specialization.

Similarly, of these same 26 social science majors one taught six periods in his minor field, five taught five periods, four taught four periods, three three periods, three two periods, one a single period, and nine interns taught no periods in their minor field. The total here is 63 class-periods taught in the minor field—the specific minor fields not identified in this case.

By the same token, three social science interns taught five periods outside their major and minor fields, two taught three periods, one taught two periods, two taught one period, and eighteen interns did no teaching outside their major and minor fields, to total 25 class-periods taught under these circumstances.

TABLE 22
Number of Interns Teaching in Major Field, Minor Field, or Neither Field During Their Year of Internship Teaching
(1958 and 1959 Groups)

Field	Number of interns	Major field								Minor field								Neither field								Intern class periods, all categories
		\multicolumn{7}{c}{Number of periods taught}	Intern class periods	\multicolumn{7}{c}{Number of periods taught}	Intern class periods	\multicolumn{7}{c}{Number of periods taught}	Intern class periods	
		6	5	4	3	2	1	0		6	5	4	3	2	1	0		6	5	4	3	2	1	0		
Soc. sci.	26	0	3	2	3	1	5	12	39	1	5	4	3	3	1	9	63	0	3	0	2	1	2	18	25	127
Life sci.	8	0	4	2	2	0	0	0	32	0	0	0	3	0	0	8	0	0	0	0	1	1	1	5	6	38
Phy. sci.	15	2	4	2	1	2	0	4	47	1	3	0	0	0	1	10	22	0	0	0	1	1	3	10	8	77
English	33	4	19	0	5	3	0	2	140	0	0	0	4	1	1	27	15	0	2	0	1	2	0	28	17	172
For. lang.	8	1	2	2	0	0	2	1	26	0	1	1	0	0	0	6	6	0	0	2	0	1	0	5	9	41
Math.	8	0	5	0	0	1	1	1	28	0	0	0	0	0	0	6	9	0	0	0	1	0	0	7	3	40
Bus. ed.	7	0	3	1	1	0	0	2	22	0	0	0	0	0	0	7	0	0	1	1	0	2	0	3	13	35
Phy. ed.	3	0	3	0	0	0	0	0	15	0	0	0	0	0	1	6	0	0	0	0	0	0	0	3	0	15
Homemaking	8	2	4	0	2	0	0	0	38	0	0	1	1	1	1	6	3	0	2	0	0	1	0	7	2	43
Not specified	6	0	1	0	0	0	0	5	5	0	0	0	1	1	0	3	9	0	0	0	1	0	1	2	14	28
Total	122	9	48	9	12	9	8	27	392 (64%)	2	10	6	8	6	5	85	127 (21%)	0	8	3	7	8	8	88	97 (15%)	616 (100%)

To summarize, the 26 social science interns taught 39 class-periods in their major field, 63 in their minor field, and 25 in neither—a total of 127 class-periods taught. Comparable data are offered in table 22 for the combined groups in the other nine major fields.

Of the 122 interns studied (both years, all fields), 27 (22 per cent) did no teaching in their major field. Conversely, 95 (78 per cent) did some teaching in their major field, that is, 9 taught six periods per day in their major, 48 five periods, 9 four periods, 12 three periods, 9 two periods, and 8 one period.

Among the three most popular teaching fields (the social sciences, English, and the physical sciences) the per cent of interns who did part of their teaching in their major field varied considerably. For example, in the social sciences, 14 of the 26 interns (53 per cent) did some teaching in their major field; in English, 31 of the 33 interns (94 per cent) did some teaching in their major field; in the physical sciences, 11 of the 15 interns (73 per cent) did some teaching in their major field. Thus, the social science majors did, proportionately, the bulk of the teaching done outside of the major field.

All interns with specialization in life sciences, physical education, and homemaking did most of their teaching in their major. For example, in the life sciences, 32 of the 38 teaching-periods (84 per cent) were spent in the major field, in physical education all of the teaching time was in the major field; and in homemaking 38 of the 43 teaching-periods (88 per cent) were in the major field. For all subject matter fields, 392 of the 616 class-periods (64 per cent) were taught in the intern's major field.

Teaching in the Minor Field

Of the 122 interns studied (both years, all fields) 85 (70 per cent) did no teaching in their minor field. Conversely, 37 (30 per cent) did some teaching in their minor field. Two taught six periods; ten taught five periods; six taught four periods; eight, three periods, six, two periods; and five taught one period in their minor field (minor field not identified.

As shown in table 22, the highest percentage of time taught by social sciences majors (63 of the 127 class-periods) was in some minor field. Life science, business education, and physical education were the only major areas where teachers did not teach in their minor. For all subject fields, 127 (21 per cent) of the 616 class-periods were taught in the intern's minor.

Teaching in Neither Major nor Minor

Of the 122 interns in the 1958 and 1959 groups, 34 (28 per cent) did some teaching outside both their major and minor. Eight taught five periods; three, four periods; seven, three periods; eight, two periods; and eight taught one period in neither their major nor minor field. For all subject areas, 97 (15 per cent) of the 616 class-periods were taught in neither the intern's major nor minor field.

The special study of teaching assignments in the 1958 and 1959 groups shows that approximately two-thirds of the intern's teaching was done in his major field, one-fifth in his minor, and one-sixth in neither.

TABLE 23

NUMBER OF DAILY PREPARATIONS FOR WHICH EACH INTERN WAS RESPONSIBLE DURING HIS YEAR OF INTERNSHIP TEACHING
(1958 and 1959 Groups)

Year	Number of preparations						Number of interns
	1	2	3	4	5	6	
1958..............	8	27	21	5	1	0	62[a]
1959..............	9	23	18	7	2	1	60
Total.........	17	50	39	12	3	1	122

[a] In the data presented in chap. iii, the number 63 has been used since this was the number of interns who entered the Program in June, 1958. During the summer session, one intern was dropped from the program; hence the data on teaching assignments were based on the 62 who taught in public schools during the 1958–1959 school year.

In view of the fact that interns were selected by the Program staff and employed by school districts, in part, because of the strength of their subject matter preparation, it is regrettable that as much as 21 per cent of their teaching assignment was in their minor field of preparation and as much as 15 per cent in neither major nor minor. How much more effective might they have been had they been given the opportunity to teach wholly the subjects which they had studied in depth?

NUMBER OF DAILY PREPARATIONS

The number of preparations for which each intern was responsible also was the subject of special study, again using the 1958 and 1959 groups. In the year 1958, the number of preparations varied from one for eight interns to five for one intern (table 23). Twenty-seven had two preparations, twenty-one had three, and five had four. The pattern for 1959 ranged from one preparation for nine interns to six for one. Twenty-three interns had two preparations, eighteen had three, seven had four, and two had five.

Comparison of the two years shows a slight increase in the average number of preparations. Whereas six interns in the 1958 group had four or more preparations, ten in the 1959 group had four or more preparations.

The variety of curriculum offerings in California's secondary schools doubtless makes it necessary for some teachers to be assigned two or more teaching fields and/or two or more courses. Major problems arise, however, when a teacher's assignments become so numerous that he is unable to devote adequate time to preparation for each teaching period.

Just how many preparations are "too many" is an open question and would obviously depend on the individual teacher, the course to be prepared for, and numerous other factors. It would be safe to say that six preparations make far too great demands on an experienced teacher and such an assignment certainly is indefensible in the case of a beginning teacher. Probably, the same statement may be said of five, four, or even three preparations.

Teaching Competence of Interns

The development of a procedure for appraising the teaching competence of interns was one of the problems first undertaken by the new Program staff early in 1956. After an extensive review of the procedures and devices mentioned in the research literature, it was decided to adopt the teacher evaluation form used by the Oakland City Schools, with some minor adaptions. The Oakland form, the staff soon learned, was the one in use in most of the school districts employing interns in the Bay Area, and it seemed prudent to use the same criteria for the Program staff's assessment of the intern's success.

This form calls for an evaluation of the teacher as outstanding, very good, good, fair, or unsatisfactory in each of the following eight areas of teacher competence:

      I. Personal characteristics
     II. Classroom control and management
    III. Teaching skills
    IV. Teacher-staff relations
     V. Extra-class activities
    VI. Academic preparation
   VII. Professional characteristics
  VIII. School-community relations

TABLE 24
EVALUATIONS OF INTERNS IN COMPARISON WITH OTHER BEGINNING TEACHERS BY DISTRICT SUPERVISORS

Year	Outstanding Number	Outstanding Per cent	Very good Number	Very good Per cent	Good Number	Good Per cent	Fair Number	Fair Per cent	Unsatisfactory Number	Unsatisfactory Per cent	None[a] Number	None[a] Per cent	Number of interns evaluated[b]
1956	8	42	7	37	3	16	1	5	0	0	0	0	19
1957	17	33	19	36	14	27	2	4	0	0	0	0	52
1958	17	29	26	44	9	15	7	12	0	0	0	0	59
1959	16	26	27	45	13	22	1	2	0	0	3	5	60
1960	19	33	22	39	12	21	3	5	0	0	1	2	57
1961	18	25	29	40	19	27	5	7	0	0	1	1	72
Total	95	30	130	41	70	22	19	6	0	0	5	1	319

[a] No evaluation made means that the school district did not return an evaluation form for a particular intern.
[b] This is the number who completed a year of internship teaching (see table 30).

The Program staff added two over-all evaluations of the intern's effectiveness to these eight more specific items: (1) competence in comparison with other beginning teachers, and (2) competence in comparison with experienced teachers (Appendix—Evaluation Form).

The person in the school responsible for the supervision of the intern—principal, assistant principal, coördinator, or department head, as the case may have been—was the one to whom the form was sent. The University subject-matter specialist in the School of Education who supervised both student teachers in the regular program and interns during the fall and spring semesters also was asked to evaluate each intern assigned to him.

An informal evaluation of each intern, using the eight areas of teacher competence, was made at the end of the first semester each year by both district and University supervisors. These evaluations were used for counseling and for the purpose of curriculum revision. At the end of the spring semester, the two over-all evaluations were secured from both district and University supervisors and these were recorded on the intern's permanent record card. The two over-all evaluations, averaged for each group of interns and for all interns, provide the data which appear in tables 24 to 29. In weighing the significance of these separate assessments of intern's teaching competence by two independent groups of appraisers, it is important to bear in mind that neither group of evaluators was a formal part of the Internship staff as such. University supervisors are subject specialists who primarily teach and supervise in the regular program. District supervisors have special responsibilities in their own school systems for the success of all beginning teachers, including interns.

Evaluation by District Supervisors

The average evaluations of school district supervisors for the 319 interns in comparison with beginning teachers were largely in the "outstanding" and "very good" categories, with 225 or 71 per cent so classified (table 24). The per cent of "outstanding" evaluations varies from 42 per cent for the 1956 (pilot) group to 25 per cent for the 1961 group. The high percentage of "outstanding" ratings for the pilot group probably is a result of the halo effect of their being the "first of their kind." The "very good" evaluations vary from 36 per cent of the 1957 group to 45 of the 1959 group. No "unsatisfactory" evaluations were given by district supervisors when comparing interns with other beginning teachers.

TABLE 25
Evaluations of Interns in Comparison with Experienced Teachers by District Supervisors

Year	Outstanding Number	Outstanding Per cent	Very good Number	Very good Per cent	Good Number	Good Per cent	Fair Number	Fair Per cent	Unsatisfactory Number	Unsatisfactory Per cent	None Number	None Per cent	Number of interns evaluated
1956	2	10	6	32	5	26	6	32	0	0	0	0	19
1957	1	2	20	38	19	37	10	19	1	2	1	2	52
1958	1	2	17	28	24	41	11	19	6	10	0	0	59
1959	3	5	17	28	29	48	8	14	0	0	3	5	60
1960	7	12	20	35	15	26	10	18	1	2	4	7	57
1961	2	3	23	32	31	43	15	21	0	0	1	1	72
Total	16	5	103	32	123	39	60	19	8	2	9	3	319

When district supervisors' average evaluations of interns in comparison with experienced teachers are examined (table 25), the following factors stand out:

1. Slightly less than four in ten of the evaluations (37 per cent) were in the "outstanding" or "very good" categories. This is considerably less than in the evaluations comparing interns with beginning teachers where 71 per cent were in these same two categories.

2. Four in ten (39 per cent) of the evaluations were in the category "good." By contrast, 22 per cent were "good" when interns were compared with experienced teachers.

3. Two in ten (19 per cent) were in the "fair" category, compared with 6 per cent of the evaluations using beginning teachers as the criteria.

4. Three per cent of the evaluations were in the "unsatisfactory" category, in contrast with none when interns were compared with beginning teachers.

5. Evaluations of "outstanding" varied from 2 per cent in the 1957 and 1958 groups to 12 in the 1960 group; "very good" from 28 per cent in 1958 and 1959 to 38 in 1957.

6. Slightly less than one-third (30 per cent) of the evaluations were categorized as "outstanding" for the total of 319, when compared with beginning teachers, while 5 per cent were so categorized when compared with experienced teachers.

It is obvious from these data that when interns are compared by district supervisors with other beginning teachers, their evaluations tend to be very high but, as might be expected, they drop considerably when related to the teaching competency of experienced teachers. It is to be noted that no comparable evaluation data are available for interns after they had taught long enough to be characterized as "experienced" teachers.

Evaluations by University Supervisors

As shown in table 26, University supervisors' evaluations are quite similar to those of district supervisors when interns are compared with beginning teachers, that is, 67 per cent "outstanding" or "very good" by University supervisors versus 71 per cent by district supervisors. Four per cent of University supervisors' evaluations were in the category "fair," and only 1 per cent, "unsatisfactory."

The evaluations of "outstanding" varied from 39 per cent of the 1960 group to 22 per cent of the 1959 group, of "very good" from 46

TABLE 26
Evaluations of Interns in Comparison with Other Beginning Teachers by University Supervisors

Year[a]	Outstanding Number	Outstanding Per cent	Very good Number	Very good Per cent	Good Number	Good Per cent	Fair Number	Fair Per cent	Unsatisfactory Number	Unsatisfactory Per cent	None Number	None Per cent	Number of interns evaluated
1958	14	24	27	46	17	30	1	1	0	0	0	0	59
1959	13	22	26	43	14	23	2	3	0	0	5	8	60
1960	22	39	22	39	10	18	2	4	0	0	1	1	57
1961	17	24	24	33	13	18	5	7	2	3	11	15	72
Total	66	27	99	40	54	22	10	4	2	1	17	7	248

[a] In 1956 and 1957 University supervisors used the "Student Teachers Appraisal of Needs and Progress" form with which they were most familiar. These evaluations, however, did not lend themselves to ready comparison with those secured on the form which school districts were using, and University supervisors also adopted and instituted the Program form, beginning with the 1958 group of interns. This fact accounts for the lack of evaluations by University supervisors in 1956 and 1957.

per cent (1958) to 33 per cent (1961). According to University supervisors, the best group of interns would appear to have been the 1960 class with 39 per cent "outstanding," 39 per cent "very good," or a total of 78 per cent in these highest categories. For the four years (1958–1961) for which there are comparable data from district supervisors as shown in table 24, they also considered the 1960 group to be excellent with 33 per cent "outstanding" and 39 per cent "very good."

Table 27 contains the average evaluations of University supervisors as they compared interns with experienced teachers. Some highlights from the table include:

1. Slightly more than 4 in 10 (42 per cent) of the evaluations were in the categories "outstanding" or "very good."
2. Slightly fewer than 4 in 10 (35 per cent) were in the category "good," 14 per cent "fair," 1 per cent "unsatisfactory."
3. Those judged "outstanding" varied from 2 per cent of the 1959 group to 18 per cent of the 1960 group; "very good" from 27 per cent of 1958 to 42 per cent of 1960.

On the whole, the similarity in the evaluations of University supervisors and district supervisors is striking.

How Competent are Interns?

An answer to the question "how competent are interns?" can be inferred from the previously cited evaluations by the two groups of evaluators—school district and University—each making independent appraisals.

Another indication of interns' teaching competence is provided by composite evaluations, using the numerical values ascribed in determining grade-point averages, that is, 4.00 = "outstanding," 3.00 "very good," 2.00 "good," 1.00 "fair," and 0.00 "unsatisfactory." The results appear in table 28 for the evaluations of district supervisors and in table 29 for University supervisors.

The data support the conclusion that both district and University supervisors agree that interns, as a group, are very good first-year teachers (average composite evaluations of 2.96 and 2.94).

When experienced teachers are the basis of comparison, intern evaluations dropped to the "good" category, and there was less agreement among the two evaluating groups. The composite figure for the evaluations by University supervisors is higher (2.41) than by district supervisors (2.18).

From the available data, it seems reasonable to conclude that interns

TABLE 27

EVALUATIONS OF INTERNS IN COMPARISON WITH EXPERIENCED TEACHERS BY UNIVERSITY SUPERVISORS

Year[a]	Outstanding		Very good		Good		Fair		Unsatisfactory		None		Number of interns evaluated
	Number	Per cent	Number	Per cent	Number	Per cent	Number	Per cent	Number	Per cent	Number	Per cent	
1958	4	7	16	27	27	46	12	20	0	0	0	0	59
1959	1	2	22	37	21	35	10	17	1	2	5	8	60
1960	10	18	24	42	18	32	2	3	0	0	3	5	57
1961	4	6	23	32	21	30	10	14	2	3	12	16	72
Total	19	8	85	34	87	35	34	14	3	1	20	8	248

[a] In 1956 and 1957, University supervisors used the "Student Teachers Appraisal of Needs and Progress" form with which they were most familiar. These evaluations, however, did not lend themselves to ready comparison with those secured on the form which school districts were using and University supervisors also adopted and instituted the Program form, beginning with the 1958 group of interns. This fact accounts for the lack of evaluations by University supervisors in 1956 and 1957.

TABLE 28
COMPOSITE EVALUATIONS OF INTERNS BY DISTRICT SUPERVISORS[a]

Composite evaluations	1956	1957	1958	1959	1960	1961	Average
With beginning teachers	3.26	2.95	2.71	3.02	3.00	2.81	2.96
With experienced teachers	2.21	2.10	1.93	2.31	2.36	2.19	2.18

[a] The composite averages were computed only on actual evaluations. The "no evaluations" were not included.

are highly valued as beginning teachers by those responsible for supervising them.

SURVIVAL DURING THE INTERNSHIP PERIOD

Some of the factors which affect the success of interns have been mentioned in this chapter; evaluation of their teaching effectiveness has been reported. A further question of importance is: what proportion of interns survived their year of internship teaching and successfully completed the Graduate Internship Teacher Education Program? In table 30, the story is told in brief. Ninety-seven per cent completed their year of internship teaching. (Two who began in June but who dropped out before the beginning of their September assignment as a teaching intern are not included.)

SUMMARY

Forty-six different school districts within a fifty-mile radius of the University have participated in the Graduate Internship Teacher Education Program. The number of districts participating has increased steadily and there has been a decided trend toward continuous participation by all coöperating districts. Interns have been assigned to 69 senior (or four-year) high schools and to 52 junior high (or intermediate) schools. There has been a decided trend to assignment of interns to four-year (or senior) high schools.

Fifty of the 333 interns were required to move from room to room one or more times during the teaching day.

TABLE 29
COMPOSITE EVALUATIONS OF INTERNS BY UNIVERSITY SUPERVISORS

Composite evaluations	1956	1957	1958	1959	1960	1961	Average
With beginning teachers	3.02	2.86	2.87	2.90	3.13	2.85	2.94
With experienced teachers	2.78	2.41	2.16	2.23	2.60	2.31	2.41

In 92 per cent of the cases, interns were assigned to teach in their major and/or minor fields at least a part of the time. A special study of the 1958 and 1959 groups showed that 15 per cent of the two groups taught outside both their major and minor fields. In the same two groups, 16 interns had four or more different daily preparations.

Interns were evaluated independently at the end of the fall and spring semesters of their year of internship teaching by two groups of personnel responsible for their supervision: (1) school district

TABLE 30

SURVIVAL DURING THE YEAR OF INTERNSHIP TEACHING

Year	Number of June entrants	Number beginning internship teaching	Number completing internship teaching	Per cent who taught successfully as interns
1956	23	22	19	86
1957	55	55	52	95
1958	63	62	59	97
1959	60	60	60	100
1960	60	60	57	95
1961	72	72	72	100
Total	333	331	319	97

personnel and (2) University subject matter specialists. The evaluations were used primarily for counseling with interns, but two annual numerical appraisals by both groups of supervisors were recorded for each intern. These evaluations were averaged for each year's group of interns and for all interns in terms of a comparison.

Both school district and University supervisors agreed in their high evaluations of interns in comparison with other beginning teachers (71 per cent and 67 per cent, respectively, of the evaluations were in the categories "outstanding" or "very good"). There was less agreement among the two groups of supervisors when interns were compared with experienced teachers, and, as might be expected, the average evaluations declined to the "good plus" category. Remarkably, only 1 per cent of intern evaluations were in the "unsatisfactory" category. From the data presented in the evaluation summaries, it would appear safe to conclude that, as a group, interns were considered by their supervisors to be highly successful beginning teachers.

Chapter VI
MOBILITY AND PERMANENCY OF INTERNS AS TEACHERS

The preparation of teachers represents considerable investment in time, money, and effort. When a fully-prepared student does not enter teaching or when the beginning teacher leaves the profession after one or two years, there is a great loss. There have been many losses of both types. It has been said that "teaching isn't a profession; it's a procession." Nationwide, the picture is far from optimistic. Only 43 per cent of the men and 66 per cent of the women who completed training for high school teaching in 1954 actually entered teaching. The average for both groups was 53 per cent. By 1956 these percentages had risen to 60 per cent for men but remained at 66 per cent for women. For both sexes, 63 per cent of the persons completing secondary credential requirements in 1956 actually entered teaching at that time.[1]

It is an expectation of the staff of the Graduate Internship Program in Teacher Education that those prepared through the Program will remain in the profession as dedicated, highly competent teachers. This hope is based on evidence gained from various screening criteria utilized in the selection of candidates for the Program (chapter ii), and from the fact that interns are older than most teacher-candidates and have had prior vocational experiences (chapter iii). Their added maturity and their delayed decision to enter teaching is presumptive evidence that they have carefully considered the advantages of teaching and that they will stay in the profession for longer periods than are common.

Is this expectation borne out by facts? What percentage of the graduates of this Program remain in teaching? Do they stay in the same school or in the same district year after year? If they move, do they move to other California school districts or to out-of-state schools? How many leave teaching careers altogether, and when do they leave?

Results of the Program's extensive follow-up studies can be shown by an overview of the present status of each group and analysis of the characteristics of those persons who have dropped out of teaching. Anyone who has engaged extensively in follow-up studies will appreciate the effort required to keep track of groups of teachers over a

[1] "The Postwar Struggle to Provide Competent Teachers," *NEA Research Bulletin*, XXXV (October, 1957).

six-year period. That this has been done in this case is due to the persistence of the staff.

MOBILITY AND PERMANENCY

Mobility

As indicated in table 31, interns show considerable mobility. As might be expected, since they finished the Program six years ago, the 1956 group has turned out to be the most mobile of the six groups, with

TABLE 31
PER CENT OF INTERNS TEACHING IN DISTRICT OF ORIGINAL EMPLOYMENT

Intern group	Duration of employment					
	Internship year	1st post-internship year	2d post-internship year	3d post-internship year	4th post-internship year	5th post-internship year
1956.........	100	81	54	30	29	25
1957.........	100	82	62	53	47	..
1958.........	100	76	62	55	..	..
1959.........	100	86	66	..	..	..
1960.........	100	96	..	..	..	..
1961.........	100	..	..	..	..	..

only one-fourth still teaching in the original district of employment. The per cent staying in the same district is 47 for the 1957 group after five years, 55 for the 1958 group after four years, 66 for the 1959 group after three years, and 96 for the 1960 group after two years.

The data in table 31 do not include mobility within a district but there was relatively little of this kind of movement. For example, in the 1958 group, 39 of the 52 who taught during their first post-internship year remained at the same school in which they had interned; while only three were transferred within the district to another school. Similarly, in the 1957 group, 28 of 39 who taught during the second post-internship year still were teaching at the same school in which they had taught the year before.

This relatively small amount of mobility provides some evidence that the "investment" which a school makes by employing an intern teacher tends to be repaid by continuity of service.

Permanency

Taken as a group, the "staying power" of interns in the profession is impressive. After six years, nearly half of the 1956 group still are teaching (table 32). Three-fourths of the 1957 and 1958 groups still are teaching after five and four years, respectively. Approximately four-fifths of the 1959 group are teaching after three years, and nine-tenths of the 1960 group after two years. No comparable data on the permanency of an institution's credentialed teachers have been published for any other group of beginning teachers.

TABLE 32
PER CENT OF INTERNS WHO REMAINED IN TEACHING

Intern group	Duration of employment					
	Internship year	1st post-internship year	2d post-internship year	3d post-internship year	4th post-internship year	5th post-internship year
1956	100	94	77	59	42	47
1957	100	93	74	79	74	..
1958	100	87	81	73	..	..
1959	100	89	79	..	..	..
1960	100	91	..	..	..	..
1961	100	..	..	..	..	..

Reasons for Leaving Teaching

A careful report of reasons for leaving teaching has been kept for each of the six classes of interns. The per cents of interns leaving teaching are shown in table 33. The reasons why interns leave teaching are much the same as those reported in drop-out studies of other beginning teachers: first, for marriage and family; second, for advanced study; third, for travel and military service. Unique perhaps to interns as a group is the small per cent leaving teaching to enter other vocations (table 33). This is understandable in view of the fact that interns are older than typical beginning teachers and have had on the average several extra years of previous vocational experience before deciding

Characteristics of Those Who Leave Teaching

The questions, who are the drop-outs and what are their distinguishing characteristics, were the subject of a special study of the 1956, 1957, and 1958 groups made at the end of the third year of the Graduate Internship Teacher Education Program and presented in a separate study.[2] The findings may be summarized as follows:

[2] "Geographic Mobility and Permanency in the Profession as Related to Selected Characteristics of Graduate Program Teachers, 1956–1959," *Research Report*, School of Education, University of California, Berkeley, II, No. 3 (November, 1960). Mimeographed.

TABLE 33
REASONS FOR LEAVING TEACHING

	1st post-internship year	2d post-internship year	3d post-internship year	4th post-internship year	5th post-internship year
1956					
Per cent teaching	94	77	59	42	47
Per cent not teaching					
Marriage and family	6	6	18	23	29
Study	0	11	6	18	6
Travel	0	6	0	0	0
Service	0	0	0	0	0
Changed vocation	0	0	6	6	6
No reason given	0	0	11	11	6
1957					
Per cent teaching	93	74	79	74	..
Per cent not teaching					
Marriage and family	2	9	9	15	..
Study	2	3	5	9	..
Travel	0	0	2	0	..
Service	0	0	0	0	..
Changed vocation	0	5	2	0	..
No reason given	3	9	3	2	..
1958					
Per cent teaching	87	81	73	..	..
Per cent not teaching					
Marriage and family	4	8	6	..	..
Study	2	11	13	..	..
Travel	2	0	2	..	..
Service	1	0	0	..	..
Changed vocation	4	0	4	..	..
No reason given	0	0	2	..	..
1959					
Per cent teaching	89	79	..	..	..
Per cent not teaching					
Marriage and family	4	8	..	..	..
Study	5	7	..	..	..
Travel	2	4	..	..	..
Service	0	0	..	..	..
Changed vocation	0	4	..	..	..
No reason given	0	0	..	..	..
1960					
Per cent teaching	91	..	..	..	..
Per cent not teaching					
Marriage and family	2	..	..	..	..
Study	3	..	..	..	..
Travel	0	..	..	..	..
Service	2	..	..	..	..
Changed vocation	2	..	..	..	..
No reason given	0	..	..	..	..

1. There was no significant relationship between the sex and number of teachers who leave.
2. Field of subject preparation and grade level taught were not related to the number of drop-outs.
3. Age was the one characteristic most closely related to the factor of leaving. All of those who dropped out were below the median age of the intern group of which they were members.
4. The drop-outs had two or fewer previous occupations.
5. They tended to be single persons, without family or children.

PROBLEMS OF INTERNS

Of the several doctoral dissertations done on various aspects of the Program, the study of Alfred Livingston is of interest here.[3] Livingston's purpose was to identify and analyze the teaching problems of interns and to compare these with those of conventionally prepared secondary school teachers in their first year.

The particular professional problems which interns, their employers and their supervisors were asked to identify were concerned with: (1) teaching, (2) relationships to pupils, (3) equipment and/or materials, (4) relationships to adults, (5) status as an intern, (6) self, and (7) orientation to the teaching profession.

The respondents also were asked to rank in order the four problems which they believed to be most pressing of those which had been identified under the several categories. In terms of problem categories, the interns mentioned classroom teaching problems twice as often as any other. Problems concerned with self were next, followed by problems which were unique to and inherent in their own particular teaching situation. As a group, the interns were relatively little disturbed by problems related to pupils.

Public school and University supervisors rated interns' problems in order as teaching, self, and relationships to pupils. The comparatively unimportant place given to problems related to pupils by interns doubtless is a result of their preoccupation with the teaching act. That this is not unusual for beginning teachers is confirmed by a study published by the Association for Student Teaching.[4] The report lists the major problems of student teachers as a need for (1) acceptance, (2)

---

[3] Alfred M. Livingston, *The Teaching Internship: The Identification and Analysis of Professional Problems of Intern Teachers* (doctoral dissertation, University of California, Berkeley, 1962).

[4] Chapter IV, "Understanding the Need of Student Teachers," *The Supervising Teacher*, 38th Yearbook of the Assoc. for Student Teaching (Dubuque, Iowa: Wm. Brown Co., Inc., 1959), p. 41.

prestige and status, and (3) self-analysis. This listing as well as those given in other studies seems to imply the same quality of personal orientation and adjustment as does the listing of intern problems.[5] The consistency which was found to exist among the problems of interns and those of regularly prepared teachers seems to mean that the professional problems of beginning teachers, including interns, are relatively persistent and universal.

By comparing these persistent and universal problems to certain characteristics of the interns, the following relationships were uncovered:

1. The age group 26–34 perceived more problems than did either the younger or the older group.

2. Women interns perceived fewer problem than men interns, indicating possibly a greater degree of relative job satisfaction on the part of the women.

3. Single interns had more problems than married interns; married interns who were parents more than those who had no children.

4. While over half the group reported having a family tradition in teaching, there was no reported difference between the family-teaching-tradition group and the no-family-teaching-tradition group in the problems they identified.

5. Interns of "blue-collar" social origin exhibited fewer problems than did those of "white-collar" social origin.

6. In terms of the Psychological Mindedness Scale and the Flexibility Scale of the California Psychological Inventory, interns scoring in the "low" interval on both scales exhibited fewer problems than did interns scoring in the "high" intervals.

Again, comparisons of these persistent and universal problems of beginning teachers with school environmental variables, revealed that:

1. Interns teaching in high schools had more problems than those assigned to junior high schools.

2. Interns teaching 152 or fewer students per day had fewer problems than those teaching 153 or more students daily.

3. Interns teaching in a school climate considered to be "ideal" or "very good" had the fewest problems. By contrast, those assigned to a school where teaching was considered to be "average" or "difficult" had many more problems.

[5] Herbert W. Wey, *A Study of the Difficulties of Student Teachers and Beginning Teachers in Secondary Schools* (doctoral dissertation, Indiana University, 1950); Edith K. Trickler, *A Study of Beginning Teachers in California High Schools* (doctoral dissertation, University of California, Berkeley, 1952); and Melvin M. Tower, "A Study of Problems of Beginning Teachers in the Indianapolis Public Schools," *Educational Administration and Supervision*, XLII (May, 1956), 261–273.

4. The social-origin of the pupils was related to the number of problems perceived—more problems were identified for interns who taught "blue-collar" pupils.

Whether interns, because they constitute a more select group than teachers generally, are more sensitive to problems or more receptive of them or more able to cope with them can only be postulated or inferred; but no information on these points is presented in the Livingston study. Perhaps some hint of the validity of the assumption can be gleaned from school administrators' comments.

SCHOOL ADMINISTRATOR'S REACTIONS

The growth of the Program and the willingness of school districts to employ interns initially and to re-employ them in competition with conventionally educated personnel must mean that school administrators have convictions about interns as teachers and about the Graduate Internship Teacher Education Program as a method of teacher preparation.

A survey was made of the 124 principals who employed one or more interns over the six-year period. Each was asked to respond candidly to such questions as:

1. Why do you employ interns in preference to conventionally prepared teacher personnel?
2. What is (and has been) your reaction to interns as beginning teachers?

TABLE 34

REASONS ADMINISTRATORS GAVE FOR EMPLOYING INTERN TEACHERS[a]

Reasons	Principals responding	
	Number	Per cent
Desire to coöperate with the University	0	0
Belief that they are the best qualified applicants available	101	81
Recognition of the Program's reputation	8	6.5
Wish to participate in "an experiment"	0	0
Need for a source of young teachers with maturity and experience	8	6.5
Desire to save on initial salary	0	0
Belief that they are easy to get rid of if they do not succeed	0	0
Recognition of the supervision provided during the first year	7	6
Total	124	100

[a] Each principal was asked to indicate the one overpowering reason.

3. In view of your experience with the Program, how would you like to see it modified or changed?

The tallied responses to the first two questions appear in tables 34 and 35. In general, the responses were highly favorable and were equally shared by principals of both junior (or intermediate) and senior (or four-year) high schools, large and small, urban or suburban.

Perhaps more significant than a statistical report of the reactions of school superintendents to these questions are excerpts from their response sheets.

An administrator who employed an intern each year for the past six years said:

I've found this program to be the best way into teaching for some very able people. Most of those that I've hired have been outstanding men and women I've found in my community and sold them on teaching via the intern program. On the whole they turned out to be among my best teachers and they've stayed with teaching once we got them over the hurdle of the internship year. I guess I'd have to say I give preference to interns. Without the Program I'd never gotten these fine people into teaching.

An administrator who has employed a large number of interns over the past six years said:

Originally we employed interns simply as a way of coöperating with Cal. But once we got to know these interns and saw how rapidly and well they developed into first rate teachers, we changed our tune. Our policy since that first year is to employ the best teachers we can find *anywhere*. That we continue to get a large number of intern teachers each year simply means that they strike us as being the best of the lot. Usually they're more mature, more committed to teaching and more enthusiastic about what's ahead of them and the preparation they've had for it.

TABLE 35
ADMINISTRATORS' REACTIONS TO INTERNS AS BEGINNING TEACHERS[a]

Reactions	Principals responding	
	Number	Per cent
Are the best beginning teachers................................	109	88
Compare favorably with other beginners.....................	10	8
Are equal to but no better or worse than others...........	3	2
Are less competent than average beginner..................	2	2
Are more trouble than they are worth........................	0	0
Total...	124	100

[a] Each principal was asked to indicate the *one* response which most clearly expressed his attitude.

A superintendent from an outlying district said:

I'd like to see things modified so I can get more interns. It's not only a good source of supply for some really talented, high-quality teachers, but it is the only source for good teachers of mathematics. I always offer more contracts than I get takers and some years I don't get any. The few I've had we like very much. They've got a sparkle most beginners I get don't have.

Just about the end of the second year, by which time they're really becoming my top teachers, they get a job in one of the big cities.

In a word, I'd like to see you devise a plan to make more of them available to us "outlanders" and require them to teach for us for a specified number of years.

A superintendent who also is the principal of a rapidly growing suburban high school district wrote:

I can answer all three of these questions best with a single response.

The first intern I hired in 1957. Today she is chairman of our foreign language department. She really knows languages—had studied abroad before we got her—and is responsible for the new language laboratory which is the envy of our neighboring districts. Parents of our top students are unhappy if they get another teacher and they let me know about it.

My second intern was a biologist from the 1958 group. He's my science department chairman, has received several summer NSF grants, and is president of our local teachers association. Now that he's finished his master's degree, I've got to fight to keep him because the nearby junior college would like to have him, too.

In 1960, we hired an intern from your MFT program. He's the best prepared beginning math teacher we've ever had. Next year when we open our second high school, I'd like to staff the school with about one-half interns and the other half with seasoned teachers.

Our '61 intern who was first in her Cal graduating class has continued to be first in most things she does as a teacher. So many people ask about her, I'm glad we long ago decided to refer to interns as beginning teachers. Explaining away such quality teachers as "interns" would be hard to do with the lay public.

If the proof of the pudding is in the tasting, then the record of the Graduate Internship Teacher Education Program is the best answer to the question of how successful it has been in preparing teachers. Over a six-year period, the interns themselves have provided the answer.

A CONCLUDING WORD

The significance of the secondary school intern program at the University of California, Berkeley, in part, can be determined by the degree to which it has achieved the purpose for which it was designed, that is, (1) to tap a new source of teacher supply, and (2) to experiment with a new design for teacher education.

On this score the evidence adduced in the preceding chapters warrants a confident affirmation of success.

Intern programs, however, have been known to come and go; to be initiated, to succeed for a time, to wane, and then to be dropped. This also *could* happen to a program as successful and acceptable as the Graduate Internship Program. For who knows what will happen when there comes to be a balance between the supply of and the demand for secondary school teachers? Will school districts then continue to employ interns when conventionally prepared, unemployed teachers by the dozens are pounding on their doors? Who knows what will happen when the Program no longer operates as an experiment with the flexibility this terms implies but instead under the more restrictive structure within which conventional programs now operate? Will the Program lose its uniqueness and thus its identity? Yes, these contingencies are all within the realm of both possibility and probability.

Despite the emphasis placed on internship programs in the new State Board of Education regulations for teacher certification, the incontrovertible fact is that conventional, not intern programs, continue to be the process by which nearly all California's teachers are prepared.

All institutions preparing teachers in California have regular programs. These, in fact, are the programs for which these colleges and universities originally were accredited (by the State Board of Education). Regular programs are the traditional curriculums for teacher preparation in which liberal arts studies, making up about 80 to 85 per cent of the total program, are supplemented in the junior, senior, or fifth years by professional studies in education, culminating in student teaching. *Conventional curriculums are the "bread and butter" programs in all institutions—the programs completed by from 85 to 100 per cent of the teacher candidates.*[1]

California's situation is not dissimilar to that in the national picture.

What does this all add up to? It adds up to a conviction by the writers that the real, long-range impact of the Graduate Internship Program will be the extent to which it has had and will continue to have an impact on conventional teacher preparation.

---
[1] James C. Stone, *California's Commitment to Public Education* (New York: Thomas Y. Crowell Co., 1961), p. 34. Italics supplied.

The influence of the Program on the conventional program has been manifold within recent years on the Berkeley campus. While it is not the purpose of this volume to detail the changes which have occurred in the regular curriculum, the simple fact is that revisions and experiments within the traditional pattern are and have been underway. The conceptual elements in these new designs are very often similar to the essential elements in the Graduate Internship Program. It is suggested that teacher educators in other institutions may well give attention to these same elements when revising and changing their traditional programs. These essential elements include:

1. A four-year liberal arts degree program with professional education reserved for the fifth year.

2. Integration of theory and practice in a professional curriculum which embodies institution-school district coöperation.

3. A team or "package" approach to teaching and supervision throughout the entire professional sequence.

4. A reorganization of professional content along some other basis than compartmentalization of separate courses taught by separate instructors.

5. High academic, personal, and professional standards for admission to and retention in the program.

The Graduate Internship Program has proved the workability and the effectiveness of a program which incorporates these elements.

APPENDIX

TABLE A-1
SENIOR OR FOUR-YEAR HIGH SCHOOLS TO WHICH INTERNS WERE ASSIGNED[a]

Schools	1956	1957	1958	1959	1960	1961	Total
Acalanes UHSD							
Acalanes					2		2
Las Lomas		1					1
Miramonte					1		1
Alameda Unif. SD							
Alameda	1	1	3	1	1	1	8
Encinal					2		2
Albany Unif. SD							
Albany	1			1	2		4
Alhambra UHSD							
Alhambra		1	1			1	3
Amador Valley Joint UHSD							
Amador Valley	1		2	1		1	5
Antioch Unif. SD							
Antioch	1		1	1	2		5
Berkeley Unif. SD							
Berkeley		3	1	6	3	3	16
Campbell Unif. SD							
Blackford						1	1
Campbell						1	1
Hayward UHSD							
Arroyo		2	1	1	2		6
Castro Valley			1	1	1	1	4
Hayward	1	2					3
Mt. Eden					1	1	2
San Lorenzo	2		1				3
Sunset					3	1	4
Tennyson			1	2			3
Jefferson UHSD							
Terra Nova						1	1
Liberty UHSD							
Liberty		1					1
Livermore Joint UHSD							
Livermore			1	1		3	5
Mt. Diablo Unif. SD							
Clayton Valley			2	1		2	5
College Park					1		1
Mt. Diablo		1			1		2
Pacifica						2	2
Pleasant Hill		1	1	2	2		6
Mt. View UHSD							
Awalt						1	1
Mt. View			1			1	2
Novato Unif. SD							
Novato					1	1	2
Oakland Unif. SD							
Castlemont		2	2				4
Fremont		2	1			2	5
McClymonds		2					2
Oakland		2	2	5	1		10
Oakland Technical		2	1	1	1	1	6
Skyline						1	1

TABLE A-1—Continued

Schools	1956	1957	1958	1959	1960	1961	Total
Palo Alto Unif. SD							
Cubberley.................	..	..	1	1	1	..	3
Piedmont Unif. SD							
Piedmont	1	..	2	..	1	..	4
Pittsburg Unif. SD							
Pittsburg.................	..	..	1	1	1	..	3
Richmond USD							
DeAnza..................	..	2	..	..	..	..	2
El Cerrito................	..	..	3	2	..	1	6
Harry Ells...............	..	..	..	..	..	1	1
Rio Vista Joint UHSD							
Rio Vista................	..	..	..	..	1	..	1
San Francisco Unif. SD							
Abraham Lincoln........	..	1	2	..	..	..	3
Polytechnic..............	..	1	..	..	..	..	1
George Washington.......	..	1	2	1	..	..	4
Lowell..................	..	1	1	..	..	..	2
San Leandro Unified SD							
San Leandro.............	..	..	2	2	1	2	7
San Mateo UHSD							
Aragon..................	..	..	..	..	..	2	2
Burlingame..............	..	1	..	..	..	..	1
Capuchino...............	..	..	1	..	..	1	2
Hillsdale................	..	1	1	..	..	..	2
San Mateo...............	..	..	1	2	..	..	3
San Rafael City SD							
San Rafael..............	1	1	..	1	..	3	6
Terra Linda.............	..	..	..	..	1	2	3
San Ramon Valley UHSD							
San Ramon Valley.......	..	1	1	..	1	2	5
Sequoia UHSD							
Carlmont................	..	..	..	..	..	1	1
Menlo-Atherton..........	..	..	1	..	..	..	1
San Carlos..............	..	..	..	..	..	1	1
Sequoia.................	..	1	1	1	1	..	4
Woodside...............	..	..	..	2	2	..	4
Sonoma Valley UHSD							
Sonoma Valley..........	1	1	..	2	1	2	7
South San Francisco Unif. SD							
South San Francisco......	..	..	..	..	1	..	1
John Swett UHSD							
John Swett..............	..	..	..	..	2	1	3
Tamalpais UHSD							
Sir Francis Drake........	..	1	..	1	..	1	3
Redwood................	..	..	1	..	..	2	3
Washington UHSD							
Irvington................	..	..	..	..	..	1	1
James Logan.............	..	..	..	2	1	3	6
Washington..............	..	..	2	..	..	3	5
Total 69	10	36	46	42	42	55	231

a School to which intern was assigned after completing the first summer period of training.

TABLE A-2
Junior High or Intermediate Schools to Which Interns Were Assigned[a]

Schools	1956	1957	1958	1959	1960	1961	Total
Antioch Unif. SD							
Antioch..................	..	1	..	..	..	..	1
Berkeley Unif. SD							
Burbank.................	..	..	..	..	..	1	1
Garfield.................	1	2	1	2	..	1	7
Willard..................	..	..	..	..	..	1	1
Carquinez Elem. SD							
Carquinez...............	..	1	..	1	1	..	3
Castro Valley Elem. SD							
A. B. Morris.............	..	..	1	1	..	..	2
Earl Warren.............	..	1	1	1	..	1	4
Hayward Elem. SD							
Strobridge...............	..	1	..	..	..	..	1
Irvington Elem. SD							
John Horner.............	..	..	..	..	..	1	1
Lafayette Elem. SD							
M. H. Stanley...........	..	1	1	1	1	1	5
Mt. Diablo Unif. SD							
Glenbrook...............	..	..	1	1	..	..	2
Loma Vista..............	..	1	..	..	..	..	1
Mt. Eden Elem. SD							
Rancho Arroyo..........	..	..	..	..	1	1	2
Napa City SD							
Redwood.................	..	..	..	..	..	2	2
Ridgeview...............	..	..	..	..	..	1	1
Oakland Unif. SD							
Claremont...............	1	..	..	..	..	..	1
Elmhurst................	..	1	..	..	..	..	1
Frick....................	..	..	3	1	..	..	4
Golden Gate.............	..	..	..	..	1	..	1
Alexander Hamilton.....	..	1	..	..	..	..	1
Bret Harte..............	2	..	..	..	..	..	2
Herbert Hoover.........	1	1	..	..	1	..	3
Lowell...................	1	..	..	..	1	..	2
McChesney..............	3	1	..	1	..	2	7
Montera.................	..	..	..	..	..	1	1
Roosevelt................	..	..	..	1	..	..	1
Westlake................	..	..	..	1	1	..	2
Woodrow Wilson........	..	1	..	..	..	..	1

TABLE A-2—Continued

Schools	Internship year						Total
	1956	1957	1958	1959	1960	1961	
Palo Alto Unif. SD							
Jordan.................	..	..	..	1	..	..	1
Ray Lyman.............	..	..	1	..	..	..	1
Petaluma City Schools							
Kenilworth.............	..	..	..	..	1	..	1
Petaluma...............	..	..	..	..	..	1	1
Pinole-Hercules Union Elem.							
Pinole-Hercules.........	..	..	..	..	..	1	1
Pittsburg Unif. SD							
Central................	..	..	1	..	1	..	2
Hillview...............	..	..	..	..	1	..	1
Redwood City Elem. SD							
Goodwin...............	..	1	..	..	..	..	1
Richmond USD							
Adams.................	..	..	..	..	1	..	1
Downer................	..	1	..	..	..	..	1
Walter Helms..........	1	..	..	..	..	..	1
San Francisco Unif. SD							
A. P. Giannini.........	..	..	..	..	1	..	1
San Leandro Unif. SD							
Bancroft...............	..	..	1	1	1	..	3
John Muir..............	..	2	..	1	1	1	5
San Mateo City Elem. SD							
Bayside................	..	..	..	..	1	..	1
Borel..................	..	1	1	1	1	..	4
College Park...........	..	..	1	..	..	..	1
San Rafael City SD							
James B. Davidson.....	2	..	..	..	..	..	2
South San Francisco Unif. SD							
Alta Loma.............	..	..	..	..	1	..	1
Parkway...............	..	..	..	..	..	1	1
Vallejo Unif. SD							
Franklin...............	..	1	1	..	..	..	2
Mariano Guadalupe.....	..	..	..	3	..	..	3
James Hogan...........	..	..	1	..	..	..	1
Walnut Creek Elem. SD							
Parkmead..............	..	..	..	..	1	..	1
Total 52	12	19	15	18	18	17	99

a School to which intern was assigned after completing the first summer period of training.

EVALUATION FORM

Teacher..................................
School...................................
Principal................................
Date.....................................

Graduate Internship Program
in Teacher Education
University of California
Berkeley, California

EVALUATION OF GRADUATE PROGRAM TEACHER COMPETENCY

This evaluation guide sketches a broad framework with eight specific areas and over-all evaluations, which may be used in considering teacher competency. The eight areas are: personal characteristics, classroom control and management, teaching skills, teacher-staff relationships, extra-class activities, academic preparation, professional characteristics, and school-community relations. The over-all evaluation asks for rank among other beginning teachers, rank among experienced teachers, and an estimate of the nature of the teaching situation in which the teacher is working.

The key item in each competency area is identified by an italicized heading. Illustrative sub items help define these key items. Comments are invited though not requested.

I. *Personal characteristics of the teacher*

Illustrative items which may be considered are:
  Physical, mental, and emotional health.
  Grooming and dress.
  Voice and use of good English.
  Friendliness, sympathy, and tact.
  Enthusiasm for teaching.
  Alertness, open-mindedness, "common sense."
  Ethical and moral standards.

With respect to *personal characteristics,* I would evaluate this intern as: (please circle appropriate category)

1	2	3	4	5
Outstanding	Very Good	Good	Fair	Unsatisfactory

Comments: ....
....

II. Classroom control and management

Illustrative items which may be considered are:
Handling of routine matters.
Promptness in beginning class work.
Working conditions in room.
Handling of books, tools, supplies, equipment.
Acceptance of students regardless of ability, achievement, or background.
Willingness to listen to and consider the students' viewpoints.
Assistance to students in establishing realistic work goals.
Handling of own behavior problems.
Firmness and consistency as circumstances dictate.
Opportunities for student participation and leadership.
Acceptance of different standards of behavior in different learning situations.
Encouragement of self-discipline, initiative, and responsibility in students.

With respect to *classroom control and management,* I would evaluate this intern as: (please circle appropriate category)

1	2	3	4	5
Outstanding	Very Good	Good	Fair	Unsatisfactory

Comments: ....

....

III. Teaching skills—instructional and guidance

Illustrative items which may be considered are:
Classroom atmosphere of mutual trust and respect.
Continually seeks improved ways of motivating students.
Sensitivity to needs of individual students.
Understanding of emotional and social needs of students.
Utilization of community educational resources.
Variety of student learning experiences.
Balance between student participation and lecture or exposition.
Understanding of objectives and content of what is being taught.
Students' interest in their work.
Problem-solving processes that are provided.
Student progress toward individual goals.

With respect to *teaching skills,* I would evaluate this intern as: (please circle appropriate category)

1	2	3	4	5
Outstanding	Very Good	Good	Fair	Unsatisfactory

Comments: ....

....

IV. *Teacher-staff relationships*

Illustrative items which may be considered are:
  Ability to work with all school personnel.
  Loyalty to the school's program even though suggesting changes.
  Tact and pleasantness in offering opinions or in disagreeing.
  Attitude toward work being performed in other schools.
  Promptness and accuracy in reporting.
  Observation of appropriate channels when reporting school and staff matters.
  Reactions to crises or emergencies.

With respect to *teacher-staff relationships*, I would evaluate this intern as: (please circle appropriate category)

1	2	3	4	5
Outstanding	Very Good	Good	Fair	Unsatisfactory

Comments: ....

....

V. *Extra-class activities*

Illustrative items which may be considered are:
  Acceptance of out-of-class assignments.
  Sponsorship of clubs or other activities.
  Supervision at sports events.
  Rapport with students during non-class contacts.

With respect to *extra-class activities*, I would evaluate this intern as: (please circle appropriate category)

1	2	3	4	5
Outstanding	Very Good	Good	Fair	Unsatisfactory

Comments: ....

....

VI. *Academic preparation*

Illustrative items which may be considered are:
  Variety of content appropriate to subject matter.
  Depth of understanding of subject matter.
  Vocational experience in subject(s) being taught.

With respect to *academic preparation*, I would evaluate this intern as: (please circle appropriate category)

1	2	3	4	5
Outstanding	Very Good	Good	Fair	Unsatisfactory

Comments: ....

....

VII. *Professional characteristics*

Illustrative items which may be considered are:
Efforts toward a thoughtful, well-defined personal framework of the purposes of education.
Perception of education as a continuing lifelong process.
Ability to evaluate education critically, weaknesses as well as strengths.
Participation in activities sponsored by professional organizations.
Experimentation with new and original ideas.
Continuation of professional growth through a variety of experiences.
Desire for constructive suggestions from other professional educators.
Discretion in the use of confidential information.

With respect to *professional characteristics*, I would evaluate this intern as: (please circle appropriate category)

1	2	3	4	5
Outstanding	Very Good	Good	Fair	Unsatisfactory

Comments: ....

....

VIII. *School-community relations*

Illustrative items which may be considered are:
Working relationships with parents.
Participation in PTA, Dad's Club, or similar school activities.
Participation in organizations serving the community.
Familiarization of laymen with educational programs.

With respect to *school-community relations*, I would evaluate this intern as: (please circle appropriate category)

1	2	3	4	5
Outstanding	Very Good	Good	Fair	Unsatisfactory

Comments: ....

....

You may consider other areas equally or more important than the preceding ones. Considering these, along with those enumerated in this form, please indicate your *over-all* evaluation of this teacher, both in comparison to other beginning and in comparison to experienced teachers.

Considering all factors, I would evaluate this teacher, *over-all*, as: (please circle appropriate category)

In comparison to other beginning teachers I have known during the last five years:	1 Outstanding	2 Very Good	3 Good	4 Fair	5 Unsatisfactory
In comparison to experienced teachers I have known during the last five years:	1 Outstanding	2 Very Good	3 Good	4 Fair	5 Unsatisfactory
On a five-point scale, how would you estimate the nature of the teaching assignment of this teacher—e.g., physical facilities, instructional materials, class load, or other factors?	1 Ideal	2 Very Good	3 Normal	4 Fairly Difficult	5 Extremely Difficult